A
**LIBRARY PARTNERS PRESS AWARD
WINNER**

David Coates

NON-FICTION AWARD

PRAISE FOR *Wanda Duncan*

'In Cracker Gothic, *Wanda Duncan writes about the intersections between family and place with precision, wit, and loving detail. Capturing moments that are at times humorous and at other times heartbreaking, Duncan makes spending time in the Florida swamp an unexpected, lyrical pleasure."*

— Aimee Mepham, author of "Raving Ones"

'Wanda Duncan says she s a Cracker—a rural southerner who doesn t quite know her manners, a trash talker, a teller of stories. To read this tough, lyrical, funny book is to feel as Cracker Wanda does: whacked into terrain that calls into question what you thought you d answered, but still electrifies your curiosity."

- Eric Wilson, author of AGAINST HAPPINESS

Cracker
Gothic

Cracker Gothic

a florida woman's memoir

WANDA DUNCAN

library partners press

a digital publishing imprint

Winston-Salem | North Carolina | Beaufort

A Library Partners Press Award Winner

This memoir is a work of creative nonfiction.
While the stories in this book are true, some names
and identifying details have been changed to protect
the privacy of the people involved.

ISBN 978-1-61846-071-4 (paperback)
ISBN 978-1-61846-075-2 (hardcover)
ISBN 978-1-61846-076-9 (ebook)

http://crackergothic.com

Cover designed by Jeff DeBlasio/Scribe
Title graphic by Wanda Duncan
Cover photographs courtesy of:
    Clay County Archives,
    21 Gratio Place
    Green Cove Springs, FL 32043

Original interior photos by Wanda Duncan

Interior photo used with permission: "Boat Run in Chesser's Prairie,"
26 May 1930, Box 1, Folder 3, Delma Eugene Presley Collection of South
Georgia History and Culture, 1880-1951. Zach S. Henderson Library
Special Collections, Georgia Southern University.

TEXT Forum 8/12
DISPLAY *Anaktoria* 12/16

Produced and Distributed By:
    Library Partners Press
    ZSR Library
    Wake Forest University
    1834 Wake Forest Road
    Winston-Salem, North Carolina 27106

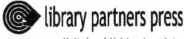 **library partners press**

a digital publishing imprint

www.librarypartnerspress.org
Winston-Salem | North Carolina | Beaufort

Manufactured in the United States of America

IN LOVING MEMORY

of

my parents

Nora Juanita Chesser Suttle

and

Alvin Marcus Suttle

WINTER IN THE NORTH.

WHERE TO GO IN FLORIDA

BY DANIEL F. TYLER

ACKNOWLEDGEMENTS

With a full and grateful heart, I would like to thank the following long-suffering individuals for their roles in nurturing my little anecdotes and stories into what is, I hope, a cohesive narrative experience.

Eric Wilson, Julie Edelson, and Tom Phillips served as the committee for my master's degree capstone project at Wake Forest University, which was the genesis of this book. All three encouraged me to continue writing, and gave me valuable ideas about form and content that stayed with me as I wrote.

Aimee Mepham picked it up as more chapters were added, imparting wise advice for seeing the big picture. Susan Schmidt of the Beaufort Writing Group combed through the little things and provided developmental guidance. Dan Lounsbury, Writing Accountability Partner Extraordinaire, generously stepped up to the plate during the final innings with contagious enthusiasm and thoughtful insights.

My children and their spouses, Alison and Becky, Will and Emily, were unfailing in their optimism and encouragement. I love you guys more than all the rocks in the world.

All of my friends—you know who you are—listened patiently to my crazy stories about Florida and never doubted that a book would emerge. Thank you.

I would have likely gone to my grave, still fiddle-farting around with this project, except Bill Kane of Library Partners Press came along, creating arbitrary deadlines, filling my inbox with official-sounding to-do lists, and insisting he would not relent until the thing was done.

And so it is.

~ Wanda Suttle Duncan, Spring 2019

The place where you were born is always chasing you.

~ Sandra Ramos, Cuban artist

ONE

There is a charm attached to the incidents of a trip upon this sheet of water that one will not soon forget.

WHITNEY'S FLORIDA PATHFINDER
FOR THE TOURIST AND INVALID, 1876

I LOAD THE CAR in the dark, drive out of my Winston-Salem neighborhood in blackness and quiet, and head south, alone. It's a trip I've made many times. I want to be on the other side of Charlotte before workday commuters begin to clog the highway, so on most trips I leave before five a.m.

After an hour, I'm passing through uptown Charlotte on Interstate 77. Skyscrapers glitter against the dark sky. The artificial glare from streetlights illuminates the gray surface of the lanes. A few cars speed along on the mostly-empty highway. In a cemetery that abuts the Interstate, granite headstones cluster in a small village. Rising on the horizon outside the city are enormous curves of metal, like cursive handwriting gone awry, reminding me of the shorthand scribbles my mother would practice on lined paper when I was a girl. As I pass closer, they resemble a graveyard of enormous serpentine skeletons in the dark: giant spirals and arching spines of the Carowinds Theme Park roller coasters. Just off the Interstate, the park is the last thing I see before the "Welcome to South Carolina" sign ahead.

An hour further, on the south side of Columbia, I cross the Congaree River. Thick, blue-gray, opaque mists hang above its broad, flat surface, backlit by the orange dawn. The river is both gloomy and serene below the concrete bridge railings. It is peaceful and enticing, and I imagine how beautiful it would be to walk along its quiet banks at dawn. But I'm traveling at eighty miles per hour with caffeine in my veins and Aerosmith blaring. I still have eight hours to drive, and there's no time to stop.

It takes just under an hour to make the southeastern diagonal cut across South Carolina on Interstate 26. Long sides of tractor-trailers shimmer with reflections from on-coming headlights. The rolling hills of the Upcountry smooth out, and the land flattens as I travel east. The early morning sun is low in the sky ahead of me.

I'm barreling toward Interstate 95, the north-south artery that will hurtle me into Florida. A friend tells me, "No one loves a road trip better than you," and he's right. I have been traveling this journey since I was a baby, a thousand-mile round trip embedded in my DNA.

My mother's ancestors settled in the Okefenokee Swamp of South Georgia before the Civil War. Later they migrated further south into Florida. My father teased my mother that her family crawled out from under a log in the Okefenokee Swamp, and there is more than a little truth to that.

My hometown, Green Cove Springs, is in North Florida. It sits on the shirttail of Georgia, about sixty miles south of the lower fringes of the Swamp. The town is one hour's drive south of the Florida-Georgia line and inland about twenty miles from the Atlantic Ocean. The name Green Cove Springs comes from the fact that the town sits in a deeply wooded cove in the elbow of the St. Johns River, with a large freshwater spring that flows into the river. Loblolly pine groves, swamp, and flat, sandy stretches of saw palmetto make up a lot of the surrounding county land.

As a young man, my father was stationed at a new naval base here during World War II. Local girls met sailors from all over the country at the USO and the theatre and the city park. My mother was one of those girls, swept off her feet by this charming young man from the North Carolina mountains. They married and started their life together in her small riverfront town. My older brother Marc and I were a new breed, a sort of half-breed that emerged in the 1950s and 60s. The products of outside blood mingled with generations of Florida Crackers, the old pioneer families of Florida, descendants of swamp dwellers.

Before Marc and I were conceived, our parents traveled the same route back and forth, seesawing between Florida and North Carolina on two-lane highways when gas was a few nickels a gallon. Our family's annual summer vacations were often spent in North Carolina, visiting my Dad's side of the family. Some of my earliest memories are of loading the car pre-dawn, riding the first hundred miles in the dark. Suitcases covered in an old quilt, situated on the back seat floorboard of our light blue 1952 Ford sedan. These were the days before seatbelts in cars, and Marc and I would stretch out in relative luxury on our backseat bed, snoozing until the bright sun cut through the windows a couple of hours into the trip.

Roadside rest stops were just pull-offs from the two-lane highways we traveled. Sometimes there would be a cluster of wooden picnic tables under oak trees, next to a gravel turnaround. The nicer picnic stops had public restrooms – usually a square cinderblock building, dead flies on the windowsills and spider webs in the corners; the words "LADIES" and "MEN" crudely stenciled in black paint on opposite sides of the building. Lunch, packed by my mother, was deviled ham and mustard sandwiches on white bread, tidy squares wrapped in waxed paper, and cans of Chek Cola from Winn-Dixie covered in ice chips in our red metal cooler.

My North Carolina grandmother lived on twenty acres of mostly wooded land with a small pond rimmed in tall cattails. Enormous granite rock outcroppings dotted her property, boulders larger than our car, some taller than a house. We climbed the big rocks, caught fireflies at the edge of the woods, skipped pebbles across the pond—all things we couldn't do in our small flat fenced backyard in Florida. When we visited at Thanksgiving, the chill in the air was delicious, the frost on the windows was magical.

Back in our den in Florida, tacked next to the black wall telephone, year after year, was the Postal Credit Union calendar. Without fail, January's photo was brilliant white and blue, a snow-covered road next to a white picket fence and a field of snow as far as you could see, under a blinding blue sky. May featured mountains of blooming azaleas. You could count on the October page being a red New England barn surrounded by blazing yellow and orange maple trees. But no matter the month, anytime I looked outside, my Florida surroundings did not look like the photographs in this calendar.

Springtime in Florida? Azaleas bloomed when Christmas decorations were barely put away. Trees, shrubs, grass were never new-green, spring-green, that bright fresh flush of new growth you see in other climates. They stayed a dull medium green most of the year. Summer? The heat, humidity, and mosquitoes started in April and lasted through October. Fall in Florida held no resemblance to the October page of the calendar. No bright colors, no piles of leaves to jump in, no cozy curl of smoke from chimneys on chilly evenings. Just a dialing-down of the summer's colors, greens turning a bit more olive. The yellows of summer faded. Trees refused to shed their leaves.

The winter scenes of the calendar were the most disheartening. Rosy-cheeked children wearing knitted caps and padded snowsuits dragged a sled across a meadow white with snow. For years I looked longingly at bright-colored snow boots in the Sears Wish Book, but never owned a pair. We Christmas caroled, house to house, in short sleeves. Shop owners sprayed white powder from aerosol cans around the edges of their front windows, as if a nice snowfall had occurred overnight in the sixty-degree weather.

I was drawn to the land where my father's roots were deep: the eastern slope of the Blue Ridge Mountains, where

Scots-Irish families intermingled and carved out a living far back in the hills. It was a region that tantalized me over many years of family trips north. The landscape was so appealing to a girl who had only known flat terrain, sandy soil, and barely discernable changes in the seasons.

At eighteen when I left for college in North Carolina, I made no plans to return to Florida. I took a direct tangent away from my small town, the stifled economy, the lack of opportunity, the boring weather, the swamps. After arriving in my college town, but before I moved into my dorm room, I insisted that my parents take me to the local DMV office so that I could get my North Carolina driver's license. I was eager to adopt this place as my new homeland. I fell in love with autumn afternoons and their glorious colors—scarlet, gold, rust-red, set against clear brilliant blue skies. Dusky evenings, the smell of smoke from actual wood-burning fireplaces. There were snowy mornings in February when campus was transformed into a magical sparkling wonderland, with the additional miracle that classes were often cancelled. April brought yellow blankets of wild daffodils across the softly rolling terrain of the Piedmont, and a full spectrum of jeweled greens from emerald to peridot to jade.

My college roommate, herself from the North Carolina mountains, saw my love of this beautiful region and declared, "You *are* a Tarheel, Wanda." I stayed, I graduated, I married. My enchantment with the beauty of this place never left me.

My father died just a few years after I graduated from college. My mother remained in our little hometown, and I became the one seesawing between North Carolina and Florida. Two more decades passed, and Mom was diagnosed with dementia. My visits increased, sometimes as often as every six weeks.

On my way south, I cross a line, my own personal threshold. It is marked by a sentinel at the precise midpoint of my journey, as my odometer hits 250 miles in. I'm still on I-26 in South Carolina, just beyond the exit for the tiny town of Bowman. In the distance I see a tall cypress tree alone in the highway median, heavily decked in Spanish moss, my first sighting of moss as I make my way south and east. It's the delineation for me between Piedmont and Coastal Plain, Upcountry and Low Country, hills and flatland. Trees with moss, trees without. Ancestral home, adopted home. I call it the Eastern Continental Moss Divide.

The habit of cypress is to spread out a broad canopy at its height, like a parasol above the other trees. And cypress is one species that moss prefers as a host. Moss is lovely and yet grotesque, exotic but creepy. Just like the South. When I pass this lone cypress, depending on the traffic, I slow down slightly, just to get a better glimpse. I've noted this tree on my trips for over ten years. I like to acknowledge it, make sure it looks healthy, that the South Carolina Department of Transportation has not selected it to come down in one of their highway-median clear-cut projects.

After I pass the Eastern Continental Moss Divide, the gray stuff hangs in trees alongside the Interstate and in the median for the rest of the trip, and I settle into the second half of my drive. There is still a good chunk of South Carolina and all of coastal Georgia to get through.

The highway moves closer to the coast, and intriguing names fly by on green highway signs, names from lost times and lost people. Coosawhatchee, Yemassee, Tullifinny, Eloree, Combahee, Eulonia. Melodious names, some with Native American and Gullah origins, now marking places to buy lottery tickets and fast food. Billboards in garish colors scream *Fireworks at Hobo Joe's! The Cheapest Cigarette Prices at the Next Exit!*

Just a few miles past the moss cypress, I take the exit from I-26 onto southbound I-95. For the remaining miles in South Carolina, the Interstate lanes snake in and out of heavy woods. Tall pines crowd both sides of the road, there are no billboards, and the shade is deep. Tree limbs stretch from the center median, hanging low over the far lane, swaying and bouncing in the updrafts created by the traffic just underneath. Traffic speeds up to eighty, eighty-five, ninety miles per hour. No exits, no cops. Most drivers who are going at least seventy-five are in the left lane, and they don't give up their places. They are in hyper-drive mode, chaining along at what is sometimes an alarming speed. It goes like this for a few miles, then the road emerges into the bright sunlight. The left-lane drivers ease off the accelerator until the next tall pine chute.

This is my favorite part of the drive. There is a rhythm to it. Vehicles pair, blend, shift in between lanes, in concert. Shadows from the tall trees fall across the pavement. The drive is smooth, the music is good. With the trees so close to both sides of the highway, the horizon ahead is a large V, the interior of the wedge filled with a promising light blue.

If it's late winter, I'm traveling alongside minivans glazed with a thin coat of dried salt spray, bearing tags from Quebec and Ontario and New Jersey and New York. Families on migration to Disney World. Bicycles cluster on the backs of motorhomes and SUVs like metal barnacles, their wire-spoked wheels spinning randomly, slowly. Trucks hauling Harley Davidson trailers pass by on their pilgrimage south to biker mecca, Daytona Beach.

I-95 is flat and straight through Georgia. On either side of the Interstate, the slash and loblolly pine stands are black-green. Pine and cypress grow together in low swamp. Sunshine occasionally cuts through the deep shaded layers of limbs, its light glimmering on the surface of the pooled water at the base of the trees. Above the wooded areas, I frequently see large birds of prey—maybe vultures, sometimes a hawk—dark silhouettes slowly pitching and wheeling against the blue.

Eventually the sky broadens as I get closer to the Florida state line. The horizon all around is low. Marshy tidal plains stretch beyond the flat Interstate bridges. Cypress trees stand along the edges of the water, and large patches of green cordgrass extend like dense carpet to the edges of the marsh. The air is thick and humid, with a brackish smell. I know that a few miles to my right, west of the Interstate, is the swamp. My swamp.

Billboards with flamingos, flip-flops and cartoon alligators promise a kitschy Florida just ahead. Far to my left along the horizon I recognize the towering boulder-shaped cumulonimbus clouds that form at the coastline from the moisture over the ocean.

Not long after crossing the state line into Florida, I peel off of I-95 north of Jacksonville, onto the beltway to circumvent the city on a wide counter-clockwise loop. I exit onto Highway 17 at the town of Orange Park. I pass the Kennel Club on the left, where greyhounds have raced on a dusty oval track for decades. On the right is McDonald's; the last time I was there was on a hot Sunday afternoon in the summer of 1985. I met a Hospice nurse who had driven down from Jacksonville. She handed me a brown paper bag with a bottle of Dilaudid pills, a powerful narcotic, and we joked about getting caught by the Orange Park police for doing a drug drop in the McDonald's parking lot. My dad was in the last horrible stages of cancer in his bed at home. I put the bag on the floor of the front seat and drove back south on 17. I never could bring myself to go back to that McDonald's.

The St. Johns River is close, parallel to Highway 17, acres of new housing developments built on the spit of land between the two. I cross Black Creek bridge. Along the right side of the bridge, the creek is lined with wooded banks and clusters of green glossy water hyacinths. On the left side of the bridge is the flat blue expanse of the St. Johns.

Just before the Green Cove Springs city limits, I pass a strip shopping center with a large vacant grocery store, a Hardee's, Pizza Hut, Dollar General, and a liquor store. Dick's BBQ where the waitresses' t-shirts once read "I prefer Dicks to Hooters," moved out a couple of years ago.

Then there's the city limit sign. My hometown, my mother's hometown, her parents' and grandparents' hometown. The pace slows, the speed limit drops. The town is a straight line of three stoplights on Highway 17, a one-mile drag where drivers have to slow down to thirty-five on their way to somewhere else. Not much has changed from last month or last year, or even from thirty years ago. Men with cane fishing poles strapped to their bikes cycle slowly on the sidewalks. Four-wheel-drive pick-up trucks rumble alongside eighteen-wheelers heading to towns further south—Palatka, Satsuma, Crescent City.

A left turn off Highway 17, then two blocks, and I am at the city park and the edge of the river. I find a parking spot and emerge from my car creaky and a little stiff from sitting all day. There's a small meandering stream with a footbridge, a playground under massive live oaks, and then there's the river: two miles wide here, a grand vista of spectacular blue water and big sky.

I walk to the city pier, turn my face into the warm sunshine and listen to the waves lap against the wooden pilings. The pier stretches out one hundred feet over the water. The river is the color of a black sapphire. A Great Blue Heron perches on a wooden dock in the distance, like a bony hunchbacked old man. Seagulls circle around the boat slips at the end of the pier.

When I left this town at eighteen, the trajectory that I planned for myself was a straight line, but my journey now resembles a spiral. I travel back and forth between my current home and my childhood home, and each trip seems to tighten something in my core. Each circle down and back feels more compelling and important; each curl deepens a place in my soul. My college roommate had it wrong. I wasn't a true Tarheel. I was an interloping half-breed Tarheel with Florida Cracker blood.

I walk back to my car and drive the remaining few blocks to my mother's house. She will be surprised to see me. Mom complains to her caregivers that I rarely visit. She greets me at the door with a bright smile, delighted that I am there, and yet confused about whether I have been gone six months or one hour. She clasps me so tightly that it breaks my heart.

Two Chesser girls and a friend, Okefenokee Swamp, 1930

TWO

Vistas were disclosed glade after glade, fringed on all sides by slender files of the cypress. The beauty was exquisite, almost supernatural.

OKEFINOKEE ALBUM, Francis Harper and Delma E. Presley, 1981

THE OKEFENOKEE SWAMP is a half million acres of primeval bog-glade. Thousands of gray-trunked cypress trees drip with lacy smoke-tinted moss. The water is the color of dark bourbon, tannin-stained, and infested with alligators. There are swamp prairies here, open expanses of water, filled with floating plants—water lilies, bladderwort, swamp iris—bordered by cypresses and tall pines. Much of the Swamp is navigable only by boat.

In the 1800s and early 1900s, the families in the Swamp lived an isolated and peculiar existence. They fished, hunted, and trapped, using an economy based on bartering, not cash. They were called Swampers and Crackers, trading animal skins and gator hides for gunpowder and cooking staples. The families kept to themselves, hidden in this mysterious deep wilderness. Instead of traveling on roads, they navigated waterways, secret channels of dark water fed from springs.

These people shared much of the same culture as the seventeenth- and eighteenth-century Scots-Irish immigrants who settled in the Appalachian Mountains. My great-great-great grandfather, William Chesser, migrated into the Swamp from western Georgia, and the family story, which varies depending on who you're talking to, is that he was fleeing a manslaughter charge. His son, my great-great grandfather, along with one of his brothers, deserted the Confederate Army and hid out in the Swamp for the duration of the Civil War.

In the 1930s, a bid was made to build a ship canal through the Okefenokee. Efforts by conservationists, including letters appealing directly to President Roosevelt, led to the Swamp being designated a wildlife refuge by Congress. The land was then protected from development, but it also became uninhabitable by the families that had lived there for generations. Firearm use was now forbidden within the refuge. Bears and wildcats decimated livestock, since the residents could not defend their own property. The families trickled away, moving back to civilization. The last holdout to leave the Swamp was Tom Chesser, who insisted on staying and raising his children the way he and his ancestors had been raised. In 1959, twenty-two years after the wildlife refuge designation, and 104 years after the first Chessers settled in the Swamp, Tom and his wife relinquished their property and moved to a nearby town.

You can explore the Swamp by kayak or canoe, but the easiest way to get an introduction to the Swamp is by guided boat tour. A ride in the covered flat-bottomed boat will take you along an old logging canal, a straight channel heavily shaded on either side for most of the tour. Ahead of the boat, nubby snouts of alligators frequently surface, pause, then silently submerge back into the dark water.

Trees heavy with vines and underbrush line the channel. Small songbirds dart among the branches; herons, buzzards, hawks float in the sky overhead.

The homestead of my ancestors still stands near the eastern rim of the Okefenokee on an island, miles from any hint of civilization, the only house remaining, on land maintained by the National Park Service. The long curving road leading to the house passes through the flat backwoods of the Swamp, hundreds of acres of pine woodland and underbrush, heavy with the spiked growth of scrub palmetto.

The house is sided in dark weathered wood with a steeply pitched metal roof and surrounded by an unpainted picket fence. There is no grass, no shrubbery near the house. The yard is a flat stretch of pale sand, swept clean and raked. Frontier families kept their yards barren and unplanted in order to reduce the hazard of fire near the house and also to prevent snakes from settling in.

The first time I visited the homestead, it was early fall, a warm and sunny day. Two park rangers wearing khaki-colored button-up shirts and brown slacks sat in rocking chairs on the front porch, eating off paper plates in their laps.

"Are you here for the Homestead Weekend?" one asked. "They're fixing a meal back in the kitchen and you're welcome to have some," he pointed his thumb over his shoulder toward the front door.

I didn't know anything about the Homestead Weekend but walked inside anyway. The structure was primitive, bare-bones. A faded feed-sack patchwork quilt covered a thin hard bed. The sandy ground under the house was visible through cracks in the floorboards. Old cans and empty, dusty blue Mason jars sat on display. The floors, the walls, the ceilings were all the same—plain, unpainted wood.

Several women were in the kitchen at the back of the house. A large stockpot full of stew simmered on the stove. Platters of fried chicken, baked beans, collard greens and biscuits were arranged on a table covered in red-and-white checked oilcloth.

I chatted with the women, explaining that I grew up in Green Cove Springs among a number of loosely connected Chesser families, and that my mother's father's family was from the Swamp. With no more information than that, one of the women broke out in a wide smile, and beamed, "You're Edna and Fred's granddaughter!"

She was correct. I was both stunned and amused. I drive forty-five miles off the interstate into a swamp, walk up to a relic of an old house, and these women stirring stew in a back room knew who I am. In some ways they know better than I do. Turns out this woman is also a Chesser, both of us descendants from the original Crackers of this Swamp.

I love going back to the quiet of the Swamp, especially in the late months of the year, when the foliage fades into muted shades of olives and browns and yellows, when the golden afternoon sunlight filters through the narrow leaves of pin oaks and mossy cedars. Reflections of trees and underbrush and sky lend the water's surface a kind of tarnished gilding. Birdsongs, like the leaf colors, are muted. Cardinals and field sparrows quietly chip and twitter in the scrub.

The house has always been empty on my return visits. No women cooking in the back, no stew simmering on the stove. Sometimes I think those women might have been ghosts. Ghosts of Cracker women enjoying a special kinship, their laughter and chatter spilling into the sandy yard, surrounding the wooden cabin hidden deep in a quiet corner of the great Swamp.

THREE

BEFORE MY MOTHER'S diagnosis, before I had the slightest clue that something was terribly amiss in her brain, I planned a trip to fly to Florida for a visit. It was April 2008, and SkyBus was the new off-price airline flying into Florida, offering flights dirt cheap, non-stop.

"I can fly down to see you now for less than it costs to drive!" Mom was happy to hear that I was coming, and we talked about eating at our favorite Chinese restaurant, making a trip to an art museum in Jacksonville, splurging on a pedicure together.

The Skybus airplane that I boarded was a brilliant orange against the clear blue Carolina sky. The flight attendants were young and playful. Their safety procedures review was more like a comedy routine. They went up and down the aisle serving snacks and selling tangerine-colored Skybus t-shirts. In the final twenty minutes of the flight, we cruised directly over barrier islands and beaches of the Atlantic coastline. Because Skybus flew into smaller airports, this flight's destination was St. Augustine, and the flight pattern was different from flights I had taken into Jacksonville. The shadow of our jet glided below us on the sand. It was the most beautiful and serene flight I had ever experienced. I was flying into a movie version of Florida, so different from the gritty all-day drive I was used to. It was the first time I ever thought about *my* Florida in a dreamy, exotic way, like you'd see in a tourism commercial. Sunny skies, palm trees, white sand beaches.

My Aunt Gerry and Uncle John met me at the airport, and we drove to Green Cove Springs. Arriving at my mother's house, the front door was closed and locked, so I knocked, waited, knocked some more. This was odd, because she usually left the door open when she was waiting for me to arrive, often standing in the doorway, watching expectantly. More knocking, then finally the door opened. There was Mom, a shocked expression on her face, holding a towel wrapped loosely around her head. Her hair was in long strands that reached her shoulders, dripping wet, white as cotton. This was a woman who visited the beauty shop religiously every Friday, kept her hair in a short style, always colored light brown.

"What are you doing here?" She pointed at her sister, accusingly. "Did you get her to come down here to check on me?" She referred to me as if I were some stranger. I had never seen her like this before.

"I've a mind to not even let you in my house! You can't come down here like this without letting me know first!"

Exchanging wide-eyed looks with my aunt and uncle, we stood at the door not knowing what to do or say, until finally Mom allowed us inside. We sat awkwardly in the tiny living room, trying to find the right words to calm my mother. Of course she knew I was coming. How could she not? I reminded her of our phone conversations, the plans we had made. She seemed to have no memory of any of it, but how could that be? Certainly she knew these things. Why was she acting like this?

The next day, things were better; she had calmed down. In fact, she never mentioned the episode at all, as if it were totally gone from her mind.

Because it was April, her taxes were due; she had her paperwork saved in an envelope on top of the television in the living room.

"I want to be sure to take this to the tax place while you're here," she said.

"What's the name of your tax preparer?"

"Oh, I don't remember his name. His office is down on Walnut Street."

I decided we would go after lunch. Dark clouds were rolling in, a typical Florida afternoon thunderstorm heading our way. We ran across her front yard in the rain to her car. A boom of thunder immediately followed a crack of lightning.

I drove the few blocks to Walnut Street. Electricity was out all over town. The traffic lights on Highway 17 were dark. Torrents of rain poured out of the sky. We rode slowly up Walnut Street, peering through what seemed like buckets of water being sloshed by the windshield wipers. I waited for Mom to point out which storefront was the tax office.

"There it is! The last one on the right!"

"Are you sure, Mom? That place looks closed."

The windows were covered with sheets of faded, torn paper. There were no signs of a business, no sign of life.

"I know that's the place. I've taken my taxes there for years!" She was annoyed, agitated. "If they were going to close, you'd think they would notify their customers!"

I circled the block one more time for good measure, but there was clearly no tax office on Walnut Street. We drove back home where I pulled out the phone book and found that H&R Block had an office north of town. I dialed the number to ask about their hours.

"We're in the shopping center with Hardee's. Yes, we can do her taxes. Happy to help." The man was very pleasant. I thanked him and hung up.

"Mom, we're going to take your taxes to H&R Block."

"Well, alright, I guess. Though I'd rather do business with local people."

The rain had subsided to a drizzle. It was already muggy, steam rising on the streets as we headed north on Highway 17.

I pulled into the shopping center. There was the green H&R Block sign. A man greeted us at the door and held it open. The office was dark.

"Our power went out about thirty minutes ago," he apologized.

He reached out to shake my mother's hand, then smiled. "Mrs. Suttle! How are you? So nice to see you again!"

I looked at her, puzzled, then at him. "Do you know my mother?"

"Oh, yes! I've done her taxes for several years!"

"Ah! Then your office was on Walnut Street?"

"No, we've never been on Walnut Street. Our office has always been here."

"How long have you been at this location?" I asked.

"I think this is our fifth year here."

When we got back to the house, I closed myself off in my mother's bedroom. I quietly called my mother's doctor and made an appointment for the next day. Something was clearly wrong, and I needed help.

When I told her that we would be going to the doctor's office, Mom was livid.

"I'll decide when I need to go to the doctor! I am perfectly healthy, and it is not your place to make these kinds of decisions for me!" She scolded me as if I were a small child.

"Mom, I think you need a check-up. I think it would be good for the doctor to talk to you."

"There is nothing wrong with me! I am *not* going to see any doctor!"

My mother, arguing with me? This was a crazy new place we had never been before. I spent five days with her. She missed the doctor's appointment because she refused to shower, refused to put on fresh clothes, refused to get in the car. We never made it to the Chinese restaurant, the museum, the pedicure.

Meanwhile, she repeated conversational topics over and over.

"Where are the neighbors who live across the street? I never see them."

"Mom, we just saw them in their driveway this morning."

"I know that! I just mean that I never see them on a regular basis."

An hour later: "Where are the neighbors who live across the street? Have they moved?"

The phone rang Friday night after supper. It was one of my local friends.

"Did you see the evening news?" he asked.

"No, why?"

"Skybus declared bankruptcy today. You might need to find another way home."

Sure enough, Skybus was no more. No more tangerine airplanes, no more fun-spirited flight crews, no more peaceful flights over the ocean. I got on the phone and found a flight back to North Carolina departing late the next night with another airline, cutting my visit short by one day. My flight took off from Jacksonville in torrential thunderstorms. The ride was bumpy, lightning flashing outside the windows the entire flight. We landed in Raleigh in the dark, rain still pouring down.

X X

I imagine many small towns have the local person who does odd jobs, runs errands, chauffeurs little old ladies to their doctor appointments and the grocery store. Maybe it's a side job, maybe it's what they do fulltime. My mother hired someone like that to help her. She always sang their praises, how wonderful this person was, so kind and thoughtful. Cleaned her house, ran errands for her. Her china closet was full of little trinkets that they bought for her at yard sales. Secondhand bird figurines, music boxes, empty cologne bottles.

After returning to North Carolina, I talked to this person on the phone, asked them to please contact me if anything seemed unusual about Mom. "Yes, I'll be happy to keep an eye on her, glad to do it." I got a phone call every few weeks after that, letting me know that Mom was fine.

I returned in October, this time having driven all day in my car. When Mom answered the door, the first thing I noticed was her hair was still white and had gotten even longer. So odd to see her look like this. Almost as if she had not been to the beauty parlor since I last saw her in April. But at least she was glad to see me, and there was none of the agitation at the front door like the last time.

I made a beeline for the bathroom; it had been a long time since my stop for gas in South Carolina. I thought it was strange that even though I let the warm water run in the sink to wash my hands, it stayed cold.

When I came out of the bathroom, a bright green hangtag on a table in the living room caught my eye. It was a second notice from the city utilities division, threatening disconnection of Mom's electricity and water because her bill was unpaid. *A second notice.* I found stacks of unopened mail in random places throughout the house. An unopened propane gas bill, unpaid and overdue. That explained the cold water. An unopened homeowner's insurance policy bill, unpaid. Her homeowner's insurance had lapsed. The pink customer copy of a statement from her cable company. She had been billed a $75 reconnection fee. Not once, but twice.

I walked out to the carport and looked at the tag on her silver Ford Taurus. The tag had expired over a year before. Her green curbside recycling bin was sitting next to the back door, filled to overflowing with nothing but empty Starbucks Frappuccino bottles. I counted them later, over one hundred and twenty bottles. In the kitchen I opened drawers and cabinets. No dishes, no glasses, no flatware. I finally found them unwashed, encrusted, and moldy, covered by a bedspread on the back porch.

I secreted her purse to the front yard where she wouldn't see me, pulled out her checkbook. Check after check made out to the person who was Mom's helper. Thousands of dollars, sometimes hundreds per day for weeks at a time. Over the previous six months, she had gone from carefully writing all checks and balancing her account, to confused entries, partial words, no amounts written in, lines skipped, and finally no entries. Her check register was like an EEG printout, showing the gradual decline of her brain activity starting at normal, but progressing through stages of dysfunction, becoming weaker, trailing off into a flat line.

I sat Mom down on the couch in the living room. When I questioned her about the checks written to the person supposedly helping her, she insisted that she had total trust in this individual. She spoke to me with a condescending tone, saying that this person had helped her for a long time, picked up prescriptions for her, cleaned her house, got money out of the bank for her.

I stopped her there. "What do you mean, 'got money'?"

Mom had handed over her bankcard and PIN, with no idea of the risk involved. I was incredulous and furious. "Mom! Your bank account could be drained and you wouldn't know it!" I couldn't control my anger, which further shut her down, making her even more defensive.

"Nobody is stealing money from me, because I get the receipts!"

"Mom, if you're paying this much money to one person, why isn't your house clean? Why are dirty dishes piled up on the back porch? Why aren't you eating hot meals instead of living off of coffee drinks?"

I spent the next week at the lawyer's office, the bank, on the phone with the police, the Sheriff's department. After reviewing a printout of Mom's checking account, the banker encouraged me to file charges. No question in her mind, this was elder abuse and fraud. When I spoke to the Sheriff, he explained that I was powerless to press charges, since there was no diagnosis of dementia prior to Mom writing the checks. I could not prove that she had written those checks under duress or with impaired judgment.

In my conversation with the police department, they offered to send out an officer who they told me specifically deals with the elderly in the community. I was back in North Carolina when he visited, so afterwards the officer called to tell me how it went.

"Your mother seems fine," he reported. "I didn't pick up on any memory issues."

I was shocked. "Did you ask her about anything current? Like what the date is? Or if she could tell you her neighbors' names, anything like that?"

"No, we just had a nice visit. I didn't want to press her or make her feel uncomfortable. She is really sweet. She told me about her grandkids, said that you worry about her too much."

I was less than one month into this nightmare, getting a crash course in how the demented mind in an elderly person works, but I was also learning how common it is for dementia to disguise itself around the people who are closest to it—family members, neighbors. And I sometimes felt like I was light years ahead of others who should have had training and knowledge in this area.

It was not too long after this that I saw a story on the national news about an elderly man in Pennsylvania who froze to death in his home. I wasn't surprised. In fact, I was somewhat jaded when I heard the news story. The neighbors stood in their front yards and told the reporter, "I talked to him across the fence every day. He was fine." Of course he seemed fine. The poor man himself probably didn't know he wasn't paying his own bills. He likely had no idea, as he stood in his yard talking to his neighbors, that there was no heat in his house and no hot water. And probably little or no food. The neighbors wouldn't know that, either, unless they bothered to go in the man's house themselves. I'd bet money he appeared perfectly normal to them, standing out in the yard, exchanging pleasantries. A person with dementia has a brain that is skilled at bluffing, in order to maintain the appearance of fitting in socially. Even if they had quizzed this man, as the doctor quizzed my mother when I finally got her to his office, his answers probably would have revealed an attempt to look normal.

"Mrs. Suttle, who is the president of the United States?"

"You mean you don't know?" She chuckled, but she didn't answer the question.

"Can you tell me what month it is?"

"Oh, I keep so busy that I don't even pay attention to the calendar anymore," Mom laughed again, dismissively.

The doctor continued patiently, kindly. "Mrs. Suttle, it's October. What holiday is coming up at the end of this month?"

"Well, there are all kinds of holidays, aren't there? Why do you want to know?"

Mom flunked the cognitive tests at the doctor's office. She could not recall three simple one-syllable words - bus, cat, door - after being asked to name them a few minutes later. On the one hand, it's what I expected. But to realize the finality of the diagnosis, to see her reduced in a sterile doctor's office among strangers, to a woman who would never again be remotely self-sufficient, was devastating.

The doctor recommended that she stay in her own home for as long as possible. "Keeping dementia patients in familiar surroundings is important. She will last longer there, so try to delay putting her in a facility as long as you can." I could tell this was a talk he had given many times over his career. "As long as she is not a risk to herself, and she doesn't show signs of wandering, I'd leave her in her home with help."

I took over every aspect of my mother's life, just short of her bodily functions, often from five hundred miles away. Her finances, the upkeep of her home, her diet, medical care, prescriptions, insurance, dental care, vision issues, her general well-being and quality of life, even the care of her dog. I constantly made educated guesses and weighed factors against one another—my mother's mental capacity, her financial situation, her medical needs. I arranged my schedule in order to drive to Florida every six to eight weeks.

I relied heavily on excellent professional caregivers who maintained daily checks, made sure she ate, managed her meds, intercepted her mail. Every day, our goal was to keep her healthy and safe in her own home and out of a facility. Every day the balance of all of the factors shifted, sometimes in her favor, sometimes not.

FOUR

The famous Green Cove Springs Mineral Spring has been known since Ponce de Leon discovered Florida. This water can be highly recommended as a drinking water of exceptional purity."

~ *A.P. Hallock, Chemist*

JUST BELOW THE SURFACE of Florida is the Floridan Aquifer. Layers of sand and rock create a unique type of water table called an artesian aquifer. Natural fissures occur, and water pushes up to the surface due to hydrostatic equilibrium, creating some 700 springs scattered across the entire state. One of those springs is in my hometown, which was originally called White Sulfur Springs in the early 1800s. It was renamed Green Cove Springs in 1866.

Juan Ponce de Leon knew something was special about the water of Florida. In 1513, he landed on the Atlantic coast, about twenty-five miles east of Green Cove Springs, where the city of St. Augustine was eventually established. He was looking for gold, but some believe he was in search of miraculous springs that reportedly brought eternal youth to the Timucua Indians. St. Augustine's historical Fountain of Youth is a tourist attraction created in the early 1900s to mark the site where Ponce de Leon came ashore. A small artesian well bubbles up there, providing a tiny trickle of water for tourists to catch in a cup and sip. But there's no proof of any connection between that well and his visit of

1513. Urban legend on our side of the St. Johns River claims the real Fountain of Youth known by the Native Americans and sought by Ponce de Leon is in Green Cove Springs.

Unlike the trickle in St. Augustine, thousands of gallons of water per minute pour from our spring, feeding directly into the adjacent city swimming pool through a channel under the surrounding pavement. This is one of the only fresh-water spring-fed municipal pools in the state, and the oldest continually operating fresh-water swimming pool in the United States.

The water exits the pool from the deep end, creating a small waterfall and a lovely meandering stream on the other side of the park. Locals refer to the stream as the "spring run." The run is shallow, with clear water flowing over the sandy bottom and through green underwater grasses. Azaleas, cypress trees, and even a small stand of banana trees line the bank of the run. Knobby cypress knees cluster at the edge of the water. It's a habitat of a species of snail, *Floridobia porterae*, not found anywhere else on earth. The spring run passes under a decorative wrought iron footbridge, then broadens and merges with the water of the St. Johns.

In the late 1800s, Green Cove Springs was known as "The Saratoga of the South," a comparison to the glamorous spas and resorts of Saratoga Springs in upstate New York. Tourist brochures called it "The Jewel of the St. Johns River." Thousands of wealthy travelers from the cold north made pilgrimages to Green Cove Springs, escaping harsh winters, heading south by steamer or locomotive. Visitors would while away the winter months in the balmy climate, believing that drinking and bathing in the sulfur water was restorative, and for some maybe even miraculous. Tourist brochures claimed that the water would cure ailments such as neuralgia, nervous prostration, Bright's Disease, rheumatism, and liver disease.

Green Cove Springs became a Victorian wonderland, a paradise with stroll ways, boardwalks, beautifully manicured flower and palm gardens. This tiny village in the swamps had eight grand resort hotels with an array of modern luxuries: electric lights, telephones, running hot and cold spring water, Turkish baths.

At the site of the current city swimming pool, there was an ornate glass-roofed spa with separate bathing areas, private dressing rooms for the wealthy, and even a casino. Local children, my grandmother among them, sold bouquets of wildflowers to tourists at the swimming pool. If there were no wildflowers to be found, they gathered small green pinecones and sold them to gullible tourists as porcupine eggs.

Green Cove Springs attracted notable visitors such as P.T. Barnum, J.C. Penney, and the Bordens of dairy fame. I've been told that Grover Cleveland ordered gallons of the spring water to be shipped to the White House when he was in office.

In the 1890s when Henry Flagler cut a swath through the swamps and built his railroad to points further south along the Florida peninsula, Green Cove Springs was forgotten. Tourists bypassed the little town on the St. Johns

River, preferring to vacation in Miami, Fort Lauderdale, West Palm Beach, the Keys. The resorts, the tourists, and the money that came with them evaporated. The spring waters were not miraculous enough to save the town.

The sulfur spring is still the centerpiece of the town's Spring Park. From a distance, it looks like a round, flat dark opal, about fifteen feet in diameter. A manmade masonry surface encircles the spring. The water is a velvety blue-green; you can see down into the spring about twenty-five feet. The beautiful shimmering surface is always gently moving. On bright days, sunbeams slice into the flowing water, creating webbed, kaleidoscopic patterns that swirl against the black craggy rocks deep in the spring. The water is heavily laced with minerals from the natural filtration through the limestone, and its temperature stays steady at seventy-eight degrees year-round. In the summer, the water is surprisingly frigid, yet in the winter it is soothingly warm. On chilly mornings, light steam hovers over the spring's surface. The rotten-egg smell of sulfur permeates the air.

One afternoon I passed a small group of people in the park walking away from the spring. Two women teetered in high heels up the sidewalk; one wore large-framed dark sunglasses with a sequined handbag clamped under her arm.

"Gawd, that stinks! How do people around here stand that? Does the whole town smell like this?" Her friends cackled.

After the group passed, I slowed down on my approach to the spring, breathed deeply and smiled. I love this smell.

I love the taste of sulfur water. Turn on a tap anywhere within the city limits, and you get water with a faint taste and odor of sulfur. The taste diminished when the city installed a chlorination system in the early 1970s. Before that, the tap water had a heavy, earthy taste, one that most natives like myself miss to this day. The spring is the only place in town where you can still get the straight jack: sulfur water unadulterated by chlorine and fluoride. It has a flavor dark and deep; you can almost chew it.

Sophisticated wine experts have a talent for detecting terroir, the geography of the grapes in a glass of wine. Their senses tell them the terrain of the land, climate, latitude where the grapes were grown. I believe water can possess the same qualities of terroir. A glass of sulfur water from this particular spring has a distinct taste and smell that resonate deep in my being. It's the taste of home.

A recent park renovation included the installation of a high safety fence around the spring. Before the city installed the fence, a number of locals visited the spring regularly in order to draw water for drinking. People would bring empty jugs and water bottles, kneel at the low concrete rim, and reach through to the water's surface to fill their containers, or simply to dip a hand into the spring.

On one occasion after the fencing was installed, I was at the spring late in the day. A young couple and elderly man were sitting on a bench at the spring, chatting. I walked a short distance away and happened to look back. The young man had scaled the fence and was perched on one of the decorative limestone boulders placed inside the fence at the spring mouth. Several empty plastic jugs were looped together with ropes hanging from his shoulders. He quickly knelt to the surface of the water, filled the jugs, handed them over the fence to the elderly man, then climbed back.

The lady with the high heels and glittery handbag couldn't stand the smell of the spring, and maybe she didn't like this shabby little town. She probably didn't take the time to walk down to where the spring run merges with the river. Didn't see the stately Great Blue Heron or the elegant white Great Egret wading gingerly in the shallows of the run. She didn't see where Bald Eagles roost in the trees overhead at sundown, or the white sandy bottom of the run where tiny minnows dart about. She will never know the history of this little town, the benefits of drinking our stinky water. Who's to say that some residents of Green Cove Springs are not actually centuries old, maintaining their youth by drinking and bathing in this water?

I should have invited that woman to my next birthday party. We'll gather around the spring, make our toasts with goblets of delicious sulfur water drawn from the *real* Fountain of Youth. And there's sure to be a big cake with lots of candles. You might be surprised to learn how old I *really* am.

As the visitor wanders through the shady streets of the town he can be but favorably impressed with the neat and tidy appearance of all he sees, miles of good sidewalk, beautiful parks, mammoth hotels, commodious churches, schools, pretty residences and lovely flower gardens, stately oakes and magnolias draped in Spanish Moss with a back ground of magnificent pine woods, all tending to make the visitor feel at home and at peace with himself and the great world in which he has his being.

POCKET DIRECTORY OF GREEN COVE SPRINGS, 1889

FIVE

THE QUI-SI-SANA HOTEL of Green Cove Springs was the
final remnant of the town's grand resort era, still standing
when I was a kid in the 1960s. The centerpiece of the town,
it overlooked the park, the swimming pool, and the river
beyond. The hotel was a fine example of Mediterranean
Revival architecture. The exterior stucco walls were a color
somewhere between ivory and coral, like a beach sky at
sunrise. It was an Italian palace tucked away in a small
southern town, with Romanesque archways, terra cotta tile
roof, and a loggia surrounding an enclosed garden full of
tropical plants. *Qui si sana* translates as "here is health," a
welcoming greeting to thousands of visitors who traveled
to Green Cove Springs seeking relief from ailments and the
bitter winters up north. By the 1970s, the Qui Si Sana had
deteriorated into a leaking, crumbling second-hand
furniture store. In the early 2000s it was bulldozed to make
way for a new city hall.

Across Highway 17 from the site of the Qui-Si-Sana is
the town's old business district. Walnut Street is still paved
in brick, with brick sidewalks on both sides of the street. It's
a one-block stretch of old storefronts, some empty, a few
open for business. A new shop sign appeared in a window,
so I stopped in one afternoon. The interior walls were
exposed brick and beams. Antique pressed-tin tiles lined
the ceiling overhead. The owner introduced herself as
Heather Harley Davidson, an artist. She was originally

Heather Davidson, and she had legally changed her name
to add "Harley." Her oversized paintings of beach scenes
and Harley-Davidson motorcycles hung throughout the
shop. The paintings had a casual breezy feel, evoking sunny
days, bright skies, the rumble of Harley engines on Highway
A1A along the beach. I went back a few times to visit
Heather's shop, but always found it closed, and eventually
the windows were empty and dark. I saw a news article
later that she had an unfortunate dust-up with law
enforcement, so I don't expect Heather to reopen anytime
soon. The article ended, rather callously, "It wasn't known
immediately if she has an attorney – or a motorcycle."

Cooter Wilson's barbershop was across the street; it's a
beauty salon now. The new owners kept some of the old
chairs, sinks, and mirrors, and when you walk in, it does feel
like you've stepped back in time fifty years or more.
Hanging on the wall is an old black and white photograph
of Cooter in his shop, along with his posted requirement
for decorum: *Thou shalt not take the Lord's name in vain.*
The other businesses from that time—a bakery, hardware
store, appliance and furniture stores, both men's and ladies'
clothing shops, a jewelry store—are all gone. It is odd to
think now how most everything anyone in the town
needed back then could be found in that one small city
block.

Following Walnut Street back across the highway, you
pass the front of the old movie theatre, the empty lot where
the town's bank used to be, and then you are at the park

and the river. Turning left on St. Johns Avenue brings you to the edge of the neighborhood where I grew up.

Immediately on the left, across from the park, is a beautiful two-story white house with a broad wraparound porch. It is one of a handful of historic homes that has been restored and maintained. In my childhood, this was the home of Sara Hallock. Mrs. Hallock was a beloved fixture in Green Cove, a woman who seemed ancient and eccentric. She rode her bicycle around town and swam every day in the city swimming pool, throughout the year. She was a throwback to the last century, taking her slow laps at the pool wearing a long swimming dress. Mrs. Hallock faithfully attended the Methodist Church, her tall slim frame always in the front pew on the left, slumping slightly as she dozed during the sermon. When the final hymn started, she would wake up and slip through a door at the front of the sanctuary, making her way to a tiny closet next to the choir loft, where she played records of organ chime hymns into a speaker system mounted on the roof of the church. Halfway across town on Sunday afternoons, you could hear the tinny, crackling tunes of *Holy, Holy, Holy* and *When I Survey the Wondrous Cross.*

One friend recalls working in the local hardware store in high school when Mrs. Hallock showed up in her customary heavy coat and pants, despite the hot weather, and purchased several gallons of paint. A few years later when she passed away, it was reported that the interior walls of the house were indeed painted in the colors she purchased, but only as high as she could reach. Every room had been painted up to about the six-foot mark, because she didn't have a ladder.

Beyond Mrs. Hallock's house, the neighborhood is a mix of small flat-roofed, cinderblock homes built in the 1950s, like the one I grew up in, and some homes from over a hundred years ago. There are homes with tidy lawns and carefully placed yard art, but there are also empty, foreclosed houses, vines creeping up abandoned screen porches and rusted-out gutters. Moss hangs on chain-link fencing and clings stubbornly to utility wires in tightly knotted gray clumps. Pickup trucks and bass boats are parked in front yards.

Even beautiful old Victorian-era homes are not immune from decay and apathy. Some appear to have been abandoned for decades, piles of junk and discarded furniture on porches and in yards. For months, a life-sized rotting stuffed polar bear lay prone behind Ionic columns on the front porch of one house. In the shadows behind the bear, a stuffed ostrich, six feet tall and listing slightly to the right, stared blankly. A porta-potty appeared for a while in a back yard, spray-painted like camouflage, swirls of brown and green and tan barely concealing the blue fiberglass sides. It sat about four feet off the ground on a structure made of wooden two-by-fours. Dual duty deer blind? Practical joke? I don't have the answer. But it does seem that code enforcement in the town has been non-existent in the last few years.

The homes in this neighborhood, some squat and unremarkable, others elegant, are linked by beautiful brick streets, laid by hand over a century ago. Branches of elegant live oak trees overhang the streets, creating vaulted cathedral ceilings of moss and ferns and dappled sunlight.

One house has intrigued me since childhood. Another Mediterranean Revival structure built in 1925 by J.C. Penney, its coral-colored stucco exterior, arched porches, and black wrought-iron trim made it seem as if a beautiful, aging flamenco dancer had come to rest in the mossy shade of the neighborhood. It is sort of a smaller version of the Qui-Si-Sana Hotel. Riding the bus in elementary school, I peered down over the wall of bamboo that encircled the lot. A small statue, a nymph-like creature, stood on a pedestal next to an old swimming pool. A sign hung over the front door of the house, foreign words in black letters. As a child, I didn't know what it said, but it added to the sense of exotic mystery, very different from other houses in the neighborhood. The original red tile roof of this beautiful home has been replaced with asphalt shingles. Plastic mini-blinds cover the windows. The wall of bamboo that encircles the perimeter of the yard has become tall and gangly, filled with moss. The sign over the front door was gone for years. There are stories about the house being haunted. The current owner told me that a restless soul can be heard walking up the hallway and through the swinging kitchen door in the dark hours of night.

I've puzzled and fretted for many years over the lack of thriving business in Green Cove Springs, the empty storefronts, the inability of some homeowners to care for their properties, the lack of interest by the city to preserve historic sites. My mother grieved, too, seeing historic buildings disappear during her lifetime. The old train depot was demolished, and decades later there is still just a flat concrete slab where it stood. The Oakland hotel, one of the resort-era buildings, toppled and cleared away, replaced by a parking lot. The Hoyt House, another beautiful Mediterranean Revival home, is still standing at least, but carved up into condominiums.

On one of my trips to Green Cove Springs, I noticed that the house-name reappeared above the front door of the old stucco home. *La Querencia* was spelled out in rustic black lettering. I looked it up. *Querencia* is Spanish for the place in a bullring where the bull retreats to regain his strength and to become centered before the next battle, a safe haven. And then I found this, a quote from author Barry Lopez: "In Spanish, *la querencia* refers to a place on the ground where one feels secure, a place from which one's strength of character is drawn...the idea itself is quite beautiful—a place in which we know exactly who we are. The place from which we speak our deepest beliefs."

SIX

And to the Tourist we would say with all honesty that a sail on the king of waters, the St. Johns, will not fail to please the most fastidious, even the chronic grumbler will see new beauties and behold wonders.

THE POCKET DIRECTORY OF GREEN COVE SPRINGS, 1889

MOM WAS WIDOWED young, at age 54. It was the early 1980s when Dad was diagnosed with inoperable cancer. His loss was devastating to her. They had been happily married for thirty-five years. Over two decades later she was diagnosed with dementia. Three years after her diagnosis, as I was actively managing Mom's life, traveling back and forth frequently between North Carolina and Florida, my husband committed suicide.

I moved mechanically through my daily routine, stunned mostly, for the first few months after Bill's death. The day-to-day details from that time are fuzzy. I returned to work. Some days I would make it for an hour or two at the office, but frequently I found myself sitting motionless in my chair, staring at my laptop, at the small blue china bowl of paperclips, at a pad of green Post-It notes, and suddenly I couldn't breathe, or had tears burning my eyes. Often, I was overcome with a vague feeling of dread, of dark weight, something nebulous but threatening. So, I would quickly pack up and bolt to my car, hoping I would not run into anyone I knew on my way to the parking lot. Some days I didn't bother going to work at all.

I was living in the city where my husband and I had raised our children, where he had a career for over twenty-five years, where we had decades-long friendships, but our kids were adults now and living in other cities. I was rattling around in an empty house, unmoored.

I found that having contact with other people, rather than being a comfort, just brought on more anxiety. Dear friends, long-time neighbors with the best of intentions hugged me, reached out, asked with a forced brightness how I was getting along. The grocery store became a place of covert operation. More than once I rerouted or aborted the trip altogether when I caught a glimpse of someone I knew rounding the corner of an aisle and possibly heading toward me. I started shopping in a store on a different side of town, often late in the evening.

I assumed, correct or otherwise, that I was the subject of conversations, whispers, speculation, and I resented it. I finally understood why people say they don't want pity. When you are pitied, that becomes your identity. You are formed in others' minds in a certain way, and you have no control over it.

My phone rang incessantly. I signed up for caller ID on my landline so that I could screen my phone calls, which is a nice way of saying I never answered the phone, nor did I return phone calls. I ignored knocks at my door. It was too draining to interact. Friends, and others who were acquaintances at best, invited me to lunch, coffee, dinner, movies. I declined most of these invitations. Devotional books in flowery gift bags were left hanging on my front doorknob by loving and concerned friends. I tossed them in my Goodwill donation bag, unopened.

A woman I barely knew wrote a note saying she wanted to "share" my grief. What could she possibly mean? That she, happy in her home, neighborhood, church, book club, country club, charity work, would like to come to my house and weep alongside me as she imagined what the death of my husband might have been like? Or imagine what my life now was like? Or what the lives of my anguished children now became? I wanted no part of her false sympathy, nor even the genuine sympathy of my real friends.

At lunch one day, a co-worker recalled a woman in their church who was widowed, and despite numerous attempts by many church members to reach out to her, the woman would not answer her phone, refused invitations; she holed up in her house and became a recluse. My co-worker pronounced very matter-of-factly, "We finally gave up. She obviously didn't want help, so everyone stopped reaching out to her."

Three months had passed since my husband's funeral. I was at a meeting on the fourteenth floor of a downtown building. During a lull, I slipped out alone into the window-lined reception area. It was October, the month of our wedding. Thirty years before, it had been a beautiful, clear-skied afternoon. The tint in the air, trees, buildings, had that magical golden glaze as we drove away from our reception, down the highway on the way to our new life. We were giddy newlyweds, and our lives ahead promised happiness, hope, adventures.

A day just like this. I gazed down over the city's skyline. The autumn light in the late afternoon was the same now as it had been in that first happy month of our new marriage. The sunlight deepened the red-orange of the brick buildings across the skyline, the light sparkled against tiny office windows and on the windshields of cars moving far below on the streets.

After our wedding we moved to this city with such excitement and happy plans so many years ago. Now sadness engulfed me to my core. I had to leave, now. Get out. Go far away. I had one place I could go. I went to my office the next day, arranged for a leave of absence, packed the car and headed south.

SEVEN

You may, at first sight, be a little disappointed. The general aspect of things is, perhaps, primitive, and somewhat strange to the Northern eye.

WHERE TO GO IN FLORIDA, Daniel F. Tyler, 1880

THIS TIME WHEN I arrived in town, I had a sense of relief, an unburdening. I could be more focused on Mom, knowing I didn't have to pack up and leave in a week. I could release my work responsibilities for a while. I had a reprieve from being in a fishbowl.

The ride from one city limit sign to the other takes only about ninety seconds. There are blocks of empty storefronts, a pawnshop, three used-car lots, two liquor stores, and five bail bondsmen offices. All that's left of several long-abandoned car dealerships are slabs of dull gray concrete, weeds growing up from the cracks. As I passed Walgreens, a young woman walked out, holding the hand of a toddler, her other arm cradling a 24-pack of Bud Light. This is the Green Cove that I remember.

Mom and Barbara, her caregiver, greeted me at the door. I had more suitcases than usual, extra boxes. Mom asked me repeatedly, "How long are you staying?" She eyed my luggage, sounding hopeful. "You're going to be with me for a while this time, right?"

I settled back into a life I eagerly escaped from thirty-five years earlier, a place that was mostly unchanged in those decades. A small old town on a river. A town whose nights are quiet, except for the whining gears of tractor-trailers passing through on Highway 17 and the horn blasts of trains. Always trains. The river is two blocks away in one direction; Highway 17 is two blocks away in the other direction, and five blocks beyond the highway are the train tracks. The same neighborhood where I rode my bike as a little girl, tagged along behind Marc and his friends when he'd let me. A little cinderblock house on a brick street, surrounded by sandspurs and crabgrass. Cell phone service was so bad that I had to stand in the front yard to make calls. Mosquitoes biting, lizards skittering, feral cats yowling. Local people fishing at the city pier every day, scarred and pitted Styrofoam ice chests and five-gallon plastic buckets strapped to their rusty bikes with bungee cords and frayed rope.

My bedroom was pale yellow, overlooking the backyard, with two big sunny windows. I pushed the bed into the corner between with the windows. I bought a bright red coverlet and a brilliant red and turquoise and yellow throw pillow for the bed. I dragged my mother's writing desk into the opposite corner, put my laptop and speakers on it, arranged for Wi-Fi installation for the house. The morning sun shone through the white sheers. This was my eighty square feet of peace and calm.

One of the things I enjoyed about having an extended stay with Mom was cooking meals for her. Living alone, I rarely cooked anymore. It felt good to make a pot of beef stew and vegetables for her, or baked chicken with a couple of sides. She tended to live off butter pecan ice cream and Lance cheese-and-peanut-butter crackers when left unsupervised. But despite how great I felt about cooking, mealtime with Mom was like battling with a stubborn toddler.

"Did you cook this? It tastes like it came from a can." She grimaced and pushed her food around on her plate. "I'm not very hungry anyway. You know I've never been a big eater. And I need to watch my figure."

I continued eating; it tasted pretty good to me. A minute or two later she would ask, frowning, "Did you make this? It doesn't have any flavor! Where's the salt shaker?" After the supper dishes were cleared, the uneaten food from her plate scraped into the trashcan, she would request a big bowl of butter pecan ice cream.

She asked for English peas, I bought English peas. We sat down to eat, English peas on our plates next to baked pork chops and mashed potatoes. Mom's first comment: "You know, I have never liked English peas."

Many times, every day, she asked if it looked like she was gaining weight. Over and over, and over, I heard the story of when she and my father were first married, he could put his hands around her waist, his fingers touching at her naval.

"How much do you weigh?" she would ask me. "Do I look like I weigh more than you? I think you've gained weight. Your dad always said that I was wasp-waisted. I've never had a big appetite, and I'm not going to start now. I need to watch my figure."

Mom had over a dozen prescription medications that I doled out throughout the day. Sometimes she swallowed her medications, and I would take the empty water glass to the kitchen sink. Before I could leave the kitchen, she would ask when she was due for her medicine.

She refused to go to bed before I turned in for the night, but then would wake me up an hour or two later, walk into my bedroom in the dark, sit on the edge of my bed and ask for pain pills. Before sunrise, she would be in my bedroom again, rubbing her joints, sometimes tears in her eyes, wanting to know if she had any medicine in the house that she could take. She was at the maximum safe dose for Hydrocodone combined with a prescription anti-inflammatory medication. It should have been enough to numb a horse. Sometimes I thought about calling a veterinarian, on the off chance that we could get better results from an equine analgesic.

More than once her voice awakened me in the middle of the night. I would find her on the phone in the living room, talking to the local police department, telling them there was a prowler, that she could hear people outside her window.

Some mornings I walked into the kitchen and found where Mom had created a barricade at the back door during the night. Trash cans, the kitchen footstool, cookie sheets, pot lids, all stacked and leaning precariously against the door, as high as she could manage. I tried to reason with her, telling her how she did not need to worry about intruders.

"Mom, no one is going to break in to the house. And besides, anyone trying to break in would just push that stuff over. It doesn't weigh enough to block the door."

"It's to make noise. It will be like an alarm," she countered.

"But, Mom, you can't hear anything!"

"What?"

Me, at the top of my voice, "YOU CAN'T HEAR ANYTHING!! You wouldn't hear it if it *did* crash to the floor."

"Then God will give me the ability to hear at just the moment that I need it."

"Maybe God could just keep the burglars away instead."

She didn't like that. She told me to quit arguing. "You are just like your dad!"

To which I blurted out, "Thank GOD, speaking of him."

I started referring to myself as a geriatric practitioner, rheumatologist, pharmacist, psychiatrist, beautician, podiatrist, dietician, veterinarian, massage therapist, chauffeur, ophthalmologist, occupational therapist. I considered the use of illegal substances, sometimes for her, sometimes for me. I'm sure I could have found someone locally to be my supplier. I decompressed by sending screaming email diatribes to friends. Lots of all-caps. Lots of profanity.

Marilyn, my best friend since third grade, came over for lunch one day. After we ate, I pulled out my laptop. I joked about coming up with decorating ideas for my room at Lowell Correctional Institute, the Florida women's prison, because I would surely end up there. "I've set up a Pinterest board where I can put ideas for decorating my prison cell at Lowell," I told her, knowing that she would understand my dark humor.

"I think Chattahoochee is a better bet for you," she countered. Chattahoochee is the old name for the Florida psychiatric hospital. "Its administration building is on the National Registry of Historic Places. Very pretty."

"If they have Wi-Fi, I could play on Pinterest all day!"

"Well, that is if the signal will work through those padded walls," she remarked, matching my sarcasm.

"I found a bedroom on Pinterest with a crystal chandelier and a padded headboard that covers the entire wall!"

"Now just check and see if they provide a sequined blue straight jacket to match those blue glitter shoes you wore at our last class reunion."

"Here's one!" I lean over and show her a glittery blue blazer on Pinterest.

"Look at that! You have gone from ranter to fashionista in no time at all!"

"I feel better already. And I haven't even picked out the chandelier for my new room yet."

"You've got all night, Sunshine," Marilyn grinned.

"If I'm in Chattahoochee, I think I'll have more than all night."

When I needed a break from the house, I could take a ten-minute walk to the city park on the riverfront. I'd go to the end of the pier, down the catwalk to the bobbing boat moorings that sway just inches above the surface of the river, surrounded by a quiet panorama of sky and water, and I would breathe. Just breathe.

I hired a sitter for my mom some evenings so I could hang out at the pool hall. I'd perch on a bar stool in a setting that was as foreign to me at first as if I were visiting another planet. Other times I'd drive to the coffee shop, get a mocha, and sit with my laptop checking work emails.

I had been at my mother's house about a month. It was November, still warm and pleasant, with sunny days and cool nights. The Great Egret waded in the spring run at the park almost every day. Customers shopped at the Family Dollar in flip-slops and shorts, where the aisles were full of red and green boxes, wrapping paper, peppermint sticks, chocolate-covered cherries, all made in China.

When my cell phone rang one afternoon, I stepped outside to the front yard to take the call. It was an officer at the Sheriff's Department back in North Carolina, a young man who was assigned to Bill's case after he committed suicide. He apologized for bothering me, asked how I was. He was calling to let me know that they were now able to release all physical effects from this case. The contents of my husband's pockets, his wedding ring. Should he mail them to me in Florida? he asked. I gave him my address and thanked him. We hung up and I went back inside.

The package arrived in a few days. It was a small padded envelope, my name and my mother's address hand-lettered, placed in the black metal mailbox next to the front door, along with Pizza Hut coupons and a Winn-Dixie sales flyer. I couldn't open it. I took it inside and placed it in the bottom of my suitcase, the one I would pack when I returned to North Carolina next month. It was far into the next year before I could bring myself to open that envelope.

There were many people from Mom's past she remembered and would ask about frequently. My kids had been out of college for years, but she still asked what they were studying, when they would graduate. She asked about her old neighbors, distant family members, many of whom had died. But she never mentioned my husband, never once asked where he was. We, her caregivers and I, had talked to Mom about it right after the suicide. She was upset initially, but it seemed the memory was now locked down in a place deeper than her other recollections. There was no way for me to know what was going on in her mind, but I believe she was aware that something was horribly wrong, she could not remember the exact details, and rather than bring up a subject that might be hurtful, she avoided it altogether. I suppose there's a physiological or neurological explanation for it, but it was also pure and simple grace. Grace for me, for her, for the two of us together in the final stages of our relationship.

EIGHT

AFTER MOM GRADUATED from Clay High School in Green Cove Springs, she was immediately hired by the school to work in the front office. Eventually she moved into the bookkeeper position, where she worked for over two decades. She spent years smoothing crumpled bills, counting out pennies and nickels and dimes, balancing hand-written spreadsheets in heavy oversized ledgers that looked like something out of a Dickens novel. The bulky metal electric adding machine on her desk resembled a typewriter, with rows of buttons across its surface, and I swear that thing weighed as much as a small car. She kept track of ticket sales from the Friday night football games, the Student Council and Future Homemakers of America treasuries, profits from the Sophomore Class car washes. At the end of every school day, she placed the monies into a heavy vinyl zippered bag, drove to the bank and dropped off her deposit at the drive-thru window.

In her later years, as her mind darkened and narrowed, she wrote out lists obsessively, mostly of her siblings. Eleven children borne by her mother. Their names, the number of years between them. The babies that died, the twins born on Christmas Day. Every caregiver, hospital or clinic nurse, physician, and visitor would hear about the eleven children. Not only did she recite the family census verbally, she tallied the names on scraps of paper, on backs of junk mail envelopes, inside the cover of the JCPenney catalog. It was a self-soothing exercise, I think. A final lifeline to her past, at a time when she had no way to recall the simplest details of her life, no way to differentiate between days, no clue what she had eaten for lunch earlier in the afternoon or whether she had even eaten at all.

Sometimes the list would have asterisks after all of the girls' names, with a footnote explaining that they all married men with double-Ts in their last names. Suttle, Suttle, Ottinger, Nettles, Crockett. Two Suttles, because Mom and one of her sisters married brothers, giving the family another interesting twist.

To this day, I still find scraps of paper with her handwriting:

1. *Frederick*
2. *Earl*
3. *Melvin*
4. *Doris and Dorothy, twins, born on Christmas Day*
5. *Barbara, "Babs," died when she was 2...*
.......and so on

Mom's other legacy in paper was her drawings. Mom was artistic, though she had no formal training. She proudly recalled how, in elementary school, the teacher asked her to draw Christmas scenes on the chalkboard in her classroom. She was good at sketching, and for a short time in my early childhood she experimented with oil paints. The only painting that remains is a waterfront scene with a sailboat and palm tree, sort of like what you'd see on a Bob Ross show, the "happy little tree" guy on PBS. But the thing she drew more than anything else was legs. Women's legs. Curvy, sexy legs, the bottom half of 1940s pin-up girls. No torsos. No heads, no arms. Some legs had dainty kitten-heel shoes, most were barefoot. On some, Mom sketched up to the waist, giving the women bathing suit bottoms, sometimes trimmed in lace or fringe. When I was growing up, it wasn't unusual to find legs sketched on papers around our house, on the back pages of the big tissue-paged phone books, on the subscription cards she would pull out of her Redbook and Good Housekeeping magazines. She continued sketching legs into her final years, until her eyesight weakened. It was one of the last things, like listing her siblings, that I believe gave her a sense of being grounded, something familiar, a physical activity that she could hold on to, and it grieved me to see the leg-sketching end.

Drawing sexy women's legs seems an unlikely activity by a shy, demure woman, a bookkeeper at the high school, and certainly not something one would expect her to do into her later years. But in talking with other friends who have experienced dementia in their older family members, I've learned the condition often decreases inhibitions and eliminates social filters. I found that there was more to Mom than just her leg-drawing.

My Mom was a beautiful woman, slim with dark hair, a lovely smile. In old photographs, she looks like a movie star. Despite her shyness, she had a fun-spirited streak that occasionally emerged, mostly at home around family. That streak came out even more when she had dementia. During my extended stays with her, it sometimes felt like we were college-aged roommates instead of elderly mother and way-past-middle-aged daughter. She frequently—and by "frequently" I mean all the time—suggested going out in order to "meet a man."

"Wanda, where can we go to meet some men? Two for me, one for you!" Then she would laugh and add, "What's that old saying? Mama used to say it. It went something like this, 'A little bit of paint and a little bit of powder, make a woman what she ain't.'" Mom recited that ditty frequently, never once getting it right so that it rhymed. She practically howled with delight when I first introduced her to the country song by Trace Adkins, "Honky Tonk Badonkadonk." She couldn't remember the name of the song, though, and so she called it the "bonkity-bonk" song. Mom overheard the phrase "drop-dead good-looking," and afterwards would often comment, "I wish I had a dead-dropping good-looking man." Well, sadly, most of the men in her age group had already dead-dropped.

We were in the waiting room at the doctor's office one day when she came across an ad in a magazine—a young man, naked, grinning, wearing only a strategically-placed banner. My mother, the shy, sweet bookkeeper, list-maker, leg-drawer, Bible-belt church-goer, held up the picture to show me, giggled mischievously, then carefully pulled the page from the magazine, folded it and placed it in her purse. Later the page showed up in the bathroom at her house, taped on the wall next to the mirror over the sink.

She complained to me about not having someone to take her out to dinner and a movie. I told her that I would take her, and she laughed me off immediately. "Not you! A man! And I don't want an old man. I want someone young and peppy." She grinned.

"Well, Mom, what age are you thinking?"

"Oh, no more than ten years, maybe fifteen years older than me at the most." She was eighty-five when she said this.

One night Mom and I were eating supper, and she asked, "Where are all the handsome men?"

"I don't know, Mom," I replied. "Wish I did."

"What are we doing wrong?" She sighed. "I guess I'm old and you're picky." She paused, with a wistful look on her face, then asked, "How's it all going to end?"

X X

I enrolled Mom for Meals on Wheels. It seemed like a great idea, a way for Mom to have some variety in her diet, along with a visit from someone in the community outside her social vacuum. The delivered meal was not a hot meal on a plate, but rather a box that resembled military rations: prepackaged imperishables, cookies, crackers, cheese. Barbara reported to me that for the most part, Mom was uninterested in the food, usually eating the cookies and tossing the rest of it in the trash. Then one morning I got a call from Barbara. She was at the house with Mom when the meal arrived, and the person standing on my mother's doorstep, holding the box of food, was the same person who had bilked her out of her money not that long ago.

And so another aspect of dementia that I was faced with, along with the medical, psychological, and financial challenges, just to name a few, was learning how hard it is to protect a person from evil-doers. Sometimes those who purport to help the elderly embed themselves into local agencies, like parasitic vermin. Perhaps they have spent years in a community where they are well known and accepted, and see an opportunity to broaden their access to their victims. In some places, this person might be caught and charged as a predator, but in other circumstances, if no one is the wiser, if safeguards are not in place, he or she may volunteer for programs that serve the elderly, enabling them to have direct contact with the elderly in their homes. Their deceit is so clever that they win accolades, a certificate to hang on the wall, a gift card for being such a wonderful volunteer. For anyone who reads this and recognizes himself or herself in this description, please know that if I am fortunate enough to outlive you, I will happily dance on your grave when you take your very special place in Hell.

NINE

The streets of Green Cove Springs deserve more than passing notice, admirably laid out with beautiful shade trees on each side, sweet scented flowers on every hand, the music of birds and all in charge of the Goddess of cleanliness who seems to have taken complete possession.

THE POCKET DIRECTORY OF GREEN COVE SPRINGS, 1889

US HIGHWAY 17 GOES through the middle of Green Cove Springs. Before the 1970s, when Interstate 95 became the gateway to Florida along the Eastern Seaboard, people traveled Highway 17, the Coastal Highway. Almost 1200 miles long, Highway 17 closely hugs the Atlantic coastline. Conventional descriptions place its origin in Punta Gorda, Florida, and its ending in Winchester, Virginia, but in my mind it runs the reverse, north to south, its origin in Virginia, its destination in Florida. To me, the significant journey, the odyssey, aims south. The highway has a website and a Facebook fan page, and you can even purchase U.S. Highway 17 t-shirts. Highway 17 chains together small communities, forgotten towns along the coastal southeast.

The major crossroad in Green Cove Springs is where Highway 17 meets Florida State Road 16. There's a bank of traffic lights, designated turn lanes. State Road 16 does not leave the state of Florida. It begins about fifteen miles east in St. Augustine, bears west across the St. Johns River to Green Cove Springs, then on toward the heart of the state for about 60 miles. Within the city limits of Green Cove Springs, State Road 16 passes two funeral homes, the old county jail, a mobile home park. At the western edge of town, the elevation rises. It's simply called "Hilltop," a small swell in the land, where the road rises momentarily, then rolls on. After passing the outlying communities beyond Hilltop, there is mile upon mile of flat, desolate scrub, high thin pine trees, straight as needles, their feet blanketed by snake-ridden palmetto thickets. The road dumps out, terminates unceremoniously, about two miles beyond the razor-wire perimeter of the Florida State Penitentiary. State Road 16 does not have a Facebook fan page.

Each day, thousands of vehicles pass through the intersection of 17 and 16. There are trucks, lots of them. Dairy-milk tankers, flat-bed semis carrying massive cast-concrete culvert piping. Drab green-and-sand-colored military vehicles chug to and from Camp Blanding, the Army camp built before World War II, twenty miles west of town. Trucks towing boats, trucks towing motorcycles; RVs the length of city busses towing cars and bikes and motorcycles.

For a short while there was a Starbucks at this intersection. The first time I saw the Starbucks, I was torn between delight and despair. Delight, because a semblance of the civilized world had arrived right here in Green Cove Springs. Despair, because I love this small town just the way it is, and I worried about what other outside influences would follow. If Starbucks now, how long before the invasion of Walmart? Cracker Barrel? Mattress stores on every corner?

The Starbucks was a chic urban oasis in a mostly rural setting. Cool furniture, indie music, vegan muffins, ethically sourced coffee beans and a rack holding a stack of the latest *New York Times*. Meanwhile, jacked-up four-wheel-drive pick-up trucks with whip antennas, gun racks, and Confederate flag decals idled at the red light just a few yards from the door. I couldn't help but wonder, does anyone ever buy a *Times* here?

If you stood just so in Starbucks and looked out the window, the green and white Starbucks logo with the smiling crowned mermaid aligned perfectly with the red and white Family Dollar sign across the street. A few years back, I wrote an essay set in the Green Cove Springs Starbucks for a creative writing group assignment. My character sipped a Venti Caramel Macchiato as tractor-trailers, heavy-duty farm trucks pulling horse trailers, and milk tankers all rumbled by. A group member offered her critique: "Starbucks coffee shops are not in that kind of setting. You don't see dairy trucks going by just outside a coffee shop window. Be more realistic."

One morning after I bought a coffee drink at Starbucks, I walked across to the Family Dollar store to pick up a few office supplies for my desk, some bathroom cleaner and toilet paper. As I passed through the home goods section, I noticed a box holding a large decorative ceramic spoon and fork. They were about fifteen inches tall, each embellished with a scene of Jesus and his disciples at the Last Supper.

The price was nine dollars. An employee, a young woman wearing a red Family Dollar apron and a nose ring, passed by as I was studying the spoon and fork.

"I love those!" she exclaimed. "I bought that same set at a flea market in St. Augustine, but my set is smaller, and it cost me sixteen dollars! That is a great price!"

She continued. "I hung them in the kitchen in our trailer. My boyfriend and I live there with my parents."

I checked out with my purchases and headed back across the parking lot. A trailer constructed from rickety plywood sheets and rusty metal bolts, hitched to a pickup truck, was parked next to my Honda. Two enormous pink pigs dozed in the sunshine, on a scattering of straw in the bed of the trailer.

I suppose my writing group critic was ultimately correct. Starbucks doesn't fit in with dairy trucks, hogs in trailers, and ceramic Jesus spoons. The Starbucks closed after about two years. The Family Dollar became a Dollar Tree, carrying the same type of merchandise in smaller sizes and even more remote off-brand labels.

After Starbucks folded, a local couple opened an independent coffee shop in the empty space at the intersection. Spring Park Coffee quickly became my favorite place to get an occasional break from being at the house. When I arrived at the coffee shop with my laptop, I would grab a table near an electrical outlet, but not too close to the window that overlooks the intersection of the two highways. I have an irrational fear that a loaded-down eighteen-wheeler will take the corner a little too fast, a little too wide, and come barreling through the wall, a spray of plate glass exploding into the shop. Even though I don't sit near the window, there is a constant blur of movement, the sunshine flashing into the shop off the sides of passing vehicles.

One afternoon I looked up and two women were walking their horses on the sidewalk outside the coffee shop. Another day a shirtless man strolled by, a snake wrapped around his upper arms and bare shoulders. If #floridaman is not from Green Cove Springs, he certainly has relatives here.

I religiously filled out the little tickets at the antique cash register every time I bought a coffee, hoping my name would be drawn for a week of free drinks. I deliberately wrote my maiden name, Suttle. I felt a pang of guilt for not writing my married name, but most people here still know me by my maiden name, and since the coffee shop relies on word of mouth to notify the winners, I figured with a surge of optimism that I'd have a better chance of finding out if I won if I used my old name.

It was a chilly, dark morning in early December. Rain had started across town before daybreak. I finished breakfast with Mom, watched her take her meds. She was settled, in a good mood.

"Mom, I'm going to run down to the coffee shop and get a drink. Do you want a hot chocolate?"

"You go on, I'll be fine. I'm going to lie down here on the couch and wait for the pain medicine to take effect. You don't have to bring me anything."

I parked at the shop, dashed through the rain. I ordered my usual, a mocha, extra shot, extra tall, extra hot. Trucks and cars filed by outside the shop windows, water spraying up onto the sidewalk from their tires. My cell phone rang; it was my friend Leigh in North Carolina. I headed back to my car with my drink.

"How's it going?" she asked.

"You know, I really like it here. I have a tiny little room, and it's so peaceful. I feel like I'm living in a monastery. There's something very Zen about it, even though I'm living with a dementia patient."

"Well, there are probably plenty of nuns in monasteries who are in various stages of dementia, so yeah, I can see how your life parallels the cloistered life!"

Over the two months of this first extended stay in Green Cove, I thought about that intersection a lot as I sat in the coffee shop, sipping my coffee, checking emails. It is only blocks away from both the place where my grandmother, mother and I were born, where my parents first met. Highway 17 always brings me into town on my trips from North Carolina; State Road 16 takes me west of town to the cemetery where my father's grave is, and where my mother's name is already carved into their joint headstone, waiting for her death date to be inscribed in the gray granite.

Many things about the town had taken on a new charm. Bumpy old brick streets, shabby houses, moss everywhere. Thoughts bubbled up quietly, much like the water emerging from the earth at the heart of town. There are friends here who never left. Other friends who made a short escape with youthful plans after high school, only to find themselves back within the city limits, their kids and grandkids attending the same schools we attended. Friends whose Friday nights are spent serving hot dogs and boiled peanuts in the concession stand during high school football games, enjoying life in this small town that held no appeal for me when I turned my back on it as a teenager.

A week before I was to leave and head back to North Carolina, my name was drawn from the big glass canister at the coffee shop. Every day that week as I drove through town, to the drugstore, the gas station, out to the cemetery, running my final errands before leaving Mom back under the watch of her caregivers, there was my name. It felt a little like being in a time warp. My unmarried name, my childhood name, in all-caps, emblazoned in yellow blinking lights on the corner of the brick building at the busy intersection of 16 and 17. It was there for all to read: every milk-truck driver, Army convoy leader, eighteen-wheeler, the Harley riders heading to the beaches of St. Augustine, the high school boys in their four-wheel drive pick-up trucks:

CONGRATULATIONS WANDA SUTTLE!
OUR CUSTOMER OF THE WEEK!
WANDA GETS A FREE COFFEE EVERY DAY FOR A WEEK!

For seven days, I stopped at that intersection many times, waiting for the light to change to green, and marveled. It was the most celebrity I had ever experienced. And I enjoyed seven delicious cups of coffee.

On my last day in town, I parked in the Walgreen's parking lot across from the coffee shop. I pulled out my phone and took pictures of my name in lights, at the crossroads of Highways 16 and 17. I had returned home and found a town unchanged, childhood friends willing to welcome me back, a place of peace and respite. And I found craziness. A small-town craziness that drew me in, that I loved immediately, that I recognized as an essential, bone-deep craziness I had forgotten, that I sorely missed. And there was so much more of it to come.

TEN

Crossroads: an intersection of two or more roads.
A point at which a crucial decision must be made
that will have far-reaching consequences.

X X

Cross: a sacred symbol in various religions worldwide,
indicating the intersection of the divine (vertical line)
with the mortal or earthly (horizontal line).
The intersection can symbolize both a place of unity
as well as a point of conflict.

X X

Etymology of the word *cross*: from Latin *crux*

X X

Crux: the decisive, pivotal point,
the essence of something,
even a source of torment or difficulty.

X X

Crux: a prominent constellation in the southern sky. Crux is the smallest of the 88 noted constellations, but is one of the most distinctive. Its name is Latin for cross, and its common name is The Southern Cross. Used by sailors for centuries in the Southern Hemisphere for navigation.

X X

Crux, the constellation, is only visible at, and south of, thirty degrees north latitude.

X X

Latitude: scope for freedom of action or thought, breathing space. Also parallel geographic coordinates circumnavigating the globe, used to measure north and south positions between the poles.

X X

Thirty-degree north latitude line: line intersecting the locations of four ancient civilizations—Babylon, Egypt, India, and China. The thirty-degree north latitude line runs through the Sphinx of Giza, Mount Everest, the likely sites of the Tower of Babel in Baghdad and the Hanging Gardens of Babylon, the Bermuda Triangle, and the Yarlung Tsangbo Canyon in China, a natural canyon larger than the Grand Canyon in the United States.

X X

"On the thirty-degree latitude line are the world's most terrible devil regions and lands of death, the most amazing coincidences and magic that cannot be explained ... magnificent seas ... quiet castles...magnificent canyons, beautiful creatures ... unpredictable mystery and beauty." *~ from the book "Mysterious Latitude 30" by Xiao Sheng, copyright 2014, translated from the original Chinese.*

X X

The thirty-degree north latitude line goes directly through Green Cove Springs, Florida.

X X

Within Green Cove Springs, 130 yards separate my childhood house and the house where I stay with my mother, and the thirty-degree north latitude line precisely bisects that space.

Al Suttle (left) and Sailors in Green Cove Springs, 1946

ELEVEN

Man is, in fact, an electromagnetic animal in every respect, living in and
surrounded by an electromagnetic environment
over which he has little control.

MAGNETISM AND ITS EFFECTS ON THE LIVING SYSTEM,
Albert Roy Davis and Walter C. Rawls, Jr.

GROWING UP IN Green Cove Springs, I never considered anything about it to be out of the ordinary. Just a typical small, quiet town, the kind of place you can't wait to get away from when you are a teenager. It was only after I came back for extended stays with my mother that I began seeing things differently. Age and distance gave me a new perspective—on the town's interesting history, the scenic beauty, the appeal of its peacefulness. But I also realized that it seemed to have more than its fair share of quirks and oddities; there was an odd undercurrent that I had never noticed. The life I took for granted growing up there was just a tad out of alignment with what's considered normal in other places. This became apparent as I occasionally shared stories with my non-Florida friends about life in Green Cove Springs. Their reactions were usually a mix of disbelief and intrigue. It was my first clue that my hometown was not your run-of-the-mill boring little burg in the boondocks.

I came across the thirty-degree latitude information after falling down a random Internet rabbit hole. There seemed to be no end to the bizarre theories connected to this latitude line: mythical ancient civilizations, astronomical influences, unexplained weather phenomenon. When I realized the line cut through Green Cove Springs, I had to investigate further.

I found a few books on Amazon.com that were specifically about the thirty-degree latitude line and its unusual reputation and history. All the books were written in Chinese, with summary descriptions in broken English. I ordered the newest one, and within a few days, it was in my hands. The title translated to "The Mysterious Latitude 30." The book was filled with photographs of the wonders of the world, things that I recognized: the Great Sphinx of Giza, the Pyramids in Egypt, Mayan ruins, Stonehenge. There were also photographs of expansive landscapes, towering mountains, massive rock formations and waterfalls. I contacted my friend Chaowei, who grew up in China, and lives in North Carolina now. I hoped he could translate some of the book for me.

When we sat down together and I pulled out the book, Chaowei grinned from ear to ear. He eagerly took the book into his hands and paged through it. "Yes! I know all about the thirty-degree latitude line!"

I showed him a map that I brought along, with the line running through Northeast Florida. "Here's my hometown. The line is right there!"

Chaowei seemed truly excited about this. "This is your hometown, the place where you were born?"

"Yep. I never knew anything about the latitude line until recently, when I came across it as I was looking up other stuff for my writing."

"That is amazing! Your town is on the line! Just like all of these other famous places!"

"So, this is a real thing in China? People know about this?" I thought the whole thing was weird.

"Oh, definitely! Chinese people are fascinated with the thirty-degree line. I had books like this when I was a kid."

He went on. "The Chinese pay attention to mountains, rivers, the natural world. They like to study what mysterious forces are at work. Forces that might influence natural occurrences, wonders in nature. And also mysterious forces behind manmade things."

He flipped through the book, scanning the text, nodding and smiling. He tapped one of the photos of a large mountain. "The Chinese idea of Feng Shui is related to this. Wind and water, natural elements, the features of the earth. Chinese people are much more attuned to these things than Westerners."

He worked his way down the table of contents with me, pointing out various topics covered in the book. While he talked, I made notes directly on the pages as quickly as I could. The book has thirty-seven chapters, divided into three headings: "Historic Tangible," "Intangible, Non-Scientific," and "Occurrences in Nature." Some items were familiar to me. Noah's Ark, the Lost City of Atlantis, the

Tower of Pisa, the Taj Mahal, the Bermuda Triangle. There were also lots of things that I had never heard of but are well known to Chaowei—a river in China that has dried up twice, the Chinese Grand Canyon, the largest Buddha statue in the world, the tallest mountain in China.

He turned to a particular page and commented, "There is a chapter here on the Bermuda Triangle, but also a chapter about China's Bermuda Triangle. It's a mysterious area in Po Yan Lake, China's largest freshwater lake. Very strange things happen there."

"But Chaowei," I interrupted him, "many of these things are not located on the thirty-degree latitude line." I already knew without looking that Stonehenge, for example, located in England, is not even close to the line.

He was unconcerned. "The Chinese think about these things with some flexibility. Maybe it is a site that is close. Maybe it is not close at all, but there is a similar occurrence that is located on the line." Honestly, my Western brain did not really understand.

But there was no questioning this: the thirty-degree line goes right through the town where I grew up. Right between the two houses that are the bookends to my life. "Do you think it means anything significant?" I asked.

He shrugged and smiled. "You should keep your eyes open. There are things there. There are forces at work. It's a mystery."

X X

I noticed a friend of mine frequently posted photos on Facebook that she had taken of her television screen during local weather forecasts—shots of the radar during thunderstorms as they moved over Green Cove Springs. The photographs were similar, taken on different days at different times. The green, yellow, orange and red blobs drifted from west to east, building from the central part of the state and moving toward the coast. But when the blobs reached the western side of the St. Johns River, where Green Cove Springs sits, a distinct bulls-eye formation came up directly over the town. The storms seemed to split around some type of unseen barrier, continue moving, and regroup beyond our town. Kathy captioned one of her photos, "The Legendary Magnetic Hole."

I was intrigued, so I asked her about the photos.

"When I was a teen, I began to notice how most storm lines would part somewhere a few miles west of the town, go north or south of Green Cove Springs, and rejoin or intensify across the river. I would say, 'Well, it lifted its skirts and jumped across the river!'"

Her family members and friends noticed the same phenomenon, and even refer to it as "the famous Green Cove Springs split." She went on to recall how when she was growing up, her family always had police, city, and county scanners, because her mother worked for the local newspaper. There were known "dead spots" in the county where signals could not transmit, including the usually reliable CB transmissions.

"Even with the new 800mhz frequency, law enforcement still has trouble from time to time with radio transmission and will operate on computers or cell phones." She continued, "Then along came paranormal shows, and they talk about limestone rock being a transmitter of magnetic frequencies. Strange things take place where limestone is. Since our town is built on limestone and limestone caverns, I always thought maybe this was the reason for the storm splits."

X X

In Green Cove Springs, the County Historical Archives are housed at the old jail. I went there one morning to do some research on the town. Driving up Walnut Street, I parked in the small visitor's lot between the old courthouse and jail.

The Clay County jail is the second-oldest jail in the state of Florida, built in 1894. On the outside of the building, a life-size model of a prisoner in a black-and-white-striped convict suit hangs by his hands from a barred upstairs window. He is crudely fashioned from what looks like papier-mâché, his limbs stiffly posed, with odd bumps and angled surfaces under the wide black and white stripes. I stood in the parking lot and stared. There was something familiar about this. It was later that I recalled a similar figure hanging from a window of the Old Jail tourist attraction in St. Augustine when I was a kid. Is this the same escapee? Did he cross the river to come hang out at our jail? Or do all historical jails in Florida have papier-mâché prisoners hanging from their windows?

In my mother's family, we had a few law officers. My uncle and great uncle both served on either the city police force or the county sheriff's department. In the 1920s, my grandfather was offered the job of city jailer, which would have included free housing for his family at the jailhouse. But my grandmother would not hear of raising children under the same roof as prisoners, so he declined.

I pulled open the door to the office and noticed a printed sign taped to the glass: "All paranormal investigators please see Vishi." Metal file cabinets lined one wall of the room, and there were glass display cases full of books and memorabilia. Vishi emerged from her small office to greet me. We chatted about the town, and I mentioned that my mother is a Chesser.

Vishi lit up. "I have a lot about the Chesser family. Do you know about Rufus Chesser?"

Unfortunately, I do know about Rufus. He was a cousin on my maternal grandfather's side of the family, with the special distinction of being sentenced to death for murder in the early 1900s in the state electric chair, affectionately known as "Old Sparky."

"I have an entire file about Rufus; he was the first man from Clay County to be electrocuted," Vishi informed me. She pulled the file. There were a dozen newspaper articles about the murder. Rufus was convicted of murdering his sweetheart Sally Boyles and his brother-in-law, in a lover's quarrel. According to one account, after he shot Sally once, she pleaded with him, "Don't shoot me again. Kiss me." He showed no mercy and continued shooting until she was dead.

He was seventeen when the crime was committed, and nineteen when he was electrocuted in 1927. Rufus sent a handwritten letter dated September 9, 1926, from his jail cell at the Florida prison in Raiford to the Clerk of Circuit Court, requesting that he be released back to Clay County. "I am suffering severely from appendicitis...I am in jail but still have feelings." I didn't see any further correspondence, and assume that the Clerk of Circuit Court showed Rufus the same mercy that Rufus showed Sally Boyles.

I made copies of some of the items in the file, then browsed through the archive room for a few minutes. A set of brass knuckles, a miniature model of both a moonshine still and a gallows, the county coroner's records, and photographs of a hanging outside the jail are just a few things on display.

As I started to leave, I pointed to the sign on the door. "What's up with the paranormal stuff?"

She was enthusiastic and at the same time very matter-of-fact. "Oh, yes! The jail is haunted. We have paranormal investigative teams here all the time."

"Do you believe in ghosts?" I asked.

"Absolutely," was her firm reply.

She reached into a desk drawer and handed me her personal business card. "C.A.P.E. – Catch Any Paranormal Event - Paranormal Investigations" was printed in Old English font. A hollow-eyed skull surrounded by red and purple flowers and a few dragonflies bordered her contact information.

"I saw a partial-body-apparition, a PBA, here one day. I'm pretty sure it was a man because of the height of it. It was a shoulder and arm, and it had on a wrinkled gray cotton shirtsleeve. When I turned my head to get a good look at it, it vanished."

She showed me her hand-held digital recorder. "You should come down here at night sometime. This is all you need. These will pick up EVPs."

The paranormal investigation profession has an entire lexicon. EVPs are electronic voice phenomena. She also talked about electromagnetic field anomalies and dust orbs. Ghost hunters come to the jail armed with all kinds of technical equipment. They film the interior cells and hallways with infrared cameras; they measure temperature changes and levels of electromagnetic energies. Enough evidence has been gathered here that the old jail has become a popular destination for ghost-seekers. At least one episode for a national paranormal television show was filmed here.

I thanked Vishi for her help and walked back to my car, glancing up at the prisoner dangling from the outside window. I tossed my file on the front seat and turned the volume up on my driving music playlist. There's nothing like Bruce Springsteen to return the universe to normal tilt.

X X

I seem to experience more than the normal amount of computer and technological malfunctions that plague all of us these days. I can shut down an electronic cash register simply by approaching the check-out lane. I wish I had kept track of all of the times I've heard a cashier say, "It was working fine until you walked up!"

I started to use the self-check-in kiosk at the airport and it froze up, with the little circle of death spinning on the screen. An airline employee stopped by to help me, commenting, "I've never seen one of these do this before!"

In one visit to the Apple Store, I managed to shut down both a laptop and an iPad, each being held by different employees. Both screens went dark, both employees had the same reaction, "I have never seen it do this before!"

"This type of thing happens to me wherever I go," I reassured one of the Apple guys.

"Maybe you're an EMF."

"What's that?"

"You know, like in science fiction movies, when someone is an electromagnetic force. It's probably your superpower."

Well, my superpower must be pretty strong. Nothing seems immune from it: cash registers, photocopiers, Bluetooth devices, apps on my phone. Probably the worst example was the time a mammogram machine shut down when I arrived at the clinic. Everyone in the waiting room had to reschedule their appointments and was sent home. I wonder if there is some connection between my EMF powers and being born on a particularly mysterious latitude line, in a place underlaid with limestone and saturated in sulfur water.

Someone who might have had an opinion about all of this, back when I was growing up, was our next-door neighbor, a scientist named Albert Roy Davis. Roy was a friendly guy, with sort of an aging James Dean look: greased-back gray hair, button-up shirts with rolled short sleeves, and a cackling laugh revealing years of smoking cigarettes. He drove a pale green convertible 50s-era Cadillac and had a Harley Davidson motorcycle. At any given time there were probably twenty cats living at Roy's house. Cats on the roof, cats asleep under the red-blooming Turks-cap bushes, cats screeching and fighting outside my bedroom window on hot, still summer nights.

When my brother was in high school, Roy hired him to do odd jobs and help out in his lab. One time I followed Marc over to Roy's. His house was a series of connected rooms that spiraled deeper and deeper inward. Unlike our house, which had no air conditioning, the rooms were chilly with a cold, sterile smell. There was clutter everywhere—lab equipment, electronic panels, cans holding wires and connectors and screws. Later I would look at the outside of his house and puzzle over how all of those rooms fit into such a small exterior.

Roy's primary research was in the field of biomagnetics, the study of magnetics produced by and applied to living things. Roy was a humanitarian. His research interests were ultimately about preventing and curing disease and illness, and finding ways to improve agricultural processes in places where there were food shortages. He held patents on various magnetic devices. Scientists from around the world visited and collaborated with Roy.

In his books, he reported on a long list of successful experiments using magnets on cancer, amputated limbs, glaucoma, broken bones, just to name a few. He claimed that using polarized water is beneficial for plants. One summer Roy planted a small plot of experimental corn in his side yard, between his house and ours. It was the biggest corn, with the biggest ears, that I have ever seen. The stalks grew taller than his house, the kernels the size of nickels.

During the height of Cold War paranoia, Roy produced and sold Radiation Fallout Kits. For $3.79, you could order a kit and measure the amount of radiation in your own backyard. The kits came in a bright yellow box and included films, filter, metal screen, and detailed instructions. Highlighted in red, plastered across the front of the box: *Your Atomic Fallout "Laboratory."*

Roy was a frequent contributor and advertiser in *The Aberree*, a newsletter published between 1954 and 1965. It claimed to be "the non-serious voice of Scientology," covering a wide range of paranormal, psychic and pseudo-scientific topics.

Here's one of Roy's ads in *The Aberree* from 1964: "Now, for the first time, you will be able to see the human aura. For months, a noted Lady Psychic from California and myself have worked to write a simple home-study course that will instruct you, step by step, on how to see the

Human Aura. $5.00 in Binder – durable cover. A first
edition. Send today, available only from us. Albert Roy
Davis, Green Cove Springs, Florida."

In an article that ran in 1963, Roy gave this first-person
account of communicating with a fellow researcher who
had died the previous year:

"One day I thought I would try to communicate with
"Bernie" by the computer, I selected a code figure, and
slowly sent a mental picture of him as I had last seen him,
and requested my guide to assist me in this
communication. At once his code figure appeared, and with
it the message: 'I am happy. I am sorry I had to leave my
dear wife, my family, and friends, but I am teaching now,
and this is what I always wanted to do.'" I am unsure what
type of computers were around in 1963 that enabled people
to communicate with the dead, but it seems to me that we
have missed some important upgrades on our current
equipment.

Roy had a tiny dark monkey named Cheetah, the kind
you see in old photographs, wearing a miniature vest and
hat, standing next to an organ grinder. It was a wiry little
thing, with bright eyes and jerky movements. Roy walked
around town with Cheetah on his shoulder, its long hairy
curled tail coiled against Roy's shirt.

One of the few terrors of my childhood was when
Cheetah escaped from Roy's house. The monkey would
scamper across the neighborhood, between houses, darting
through carports and under shrubbery. One neighbor
recalls the time that Cheetah jumped on the back of their

black Labrador Retriever and rode him around like a pony. More than once, the escaped monkey latched on to our front screen door, lunging wild-eyed, and screeching into our living room. I think he would have killed us all if he could have gotten past that door. It was terrifying.

In retrospect, it was sort of like being traumatized, as many of us were back in those days, by the creepy flying monkeys in *The Wizard of Oz.* And there's actually a fair bit of synchronicity between Green Cove Springs and Oz. Not only did we have a scary monkey, we had the pseudo-scientist (like the Wizard), the suspiciously modified crops (Dorothy's poppies, Roy's corn), and we had a real-life Munchkin.

In *The Wizard of Oz*, the Munchkin Coroner struts out, dressed in a dark robe and imposing curled-brim top hat, unrolls an official proclamation and solemnly announces the death of the Wicked Witch of the East. He was played by a three-and-a-half-foot tall gentleman named Meinhardt Raabe. Mr. Raabe was originally from Wisconsin, had a long career with the Oscar Meyer Company, and served in the Civil Air Patrol during World War II. He married Marie Hartline in 1946. Marie was also a little person, too—just three feet, ten inches tall—and had a show business background herself. When Meinhardt and Marie retired, they relocated to the Penney Farms Retirement Community just outside the city limits of Green Cove Springs. It was a common sight to see them in town, driving their station wagon and shopping together at Winn-Dixie.

Roy the scientist passed away many years ago, but I wish I could summon him with my laptop the way he called up his dead friend Bernie. I would love to hear what he has to say about EMFs, biomagnetics, human auras, ghosts at the jail, the connection between limestone and magnetic frequencies, and the mysterious thirty-degree north latitude line. Truly, there's no place like home, especially when home is Green Cove Springs.

WE INVITE YOU TO JOIN THE
FLORIDA METAPSYCHICAL ASSOCIATION TODAY

The Fastest Growing National and International Metapsychical and Astrological Group in the World.

You receive our monthly Journal on Health, Psychic Research, Science, and Medical Notes of Interest. Some of our writers are noted Authorities and are from many countries around the world.

Membership $5 a year--Subscription Journal $2 year
Send for your Membership or Subscription Today

FLORIDA METAPSYCHICAL ASSOCIATION
ALBERT ROY DAVIS, Secretary-President
GREEN COVE SPRINGS, FLA.

TWELVE

Man is a sort of semi-amphibious creature – he loves the water. Consequently one of the first things which attaches to the newcomer to Green Cove is the discovery that the whole river front is not taken up by steamboat wharves, stores and warehouses.

WHERE TO GO IN FLORIDA, Daniel F. Tyler, 1880

WHEN MY MOTHER WAS a little girl, she put two dimes in her pocket on Saturday afternoons and walked to the Clay Theatre. The new movie theatre on Walnut Street was built when she was seven years old. One dime paid for cartoons and western movies in the cool dark theater all the way till suppertime. The other dime got her a "co-cola" and a candy bar.

When I was a teenager, we called it "The Roach." By then, the theatre was in its dying days, and was musty and dark. In the 1970s, heavy, sweet clouds of pot smoke hung in the balcony on Saturday nights. Eventually, The Roach closed.

During the time that I was taking care of Mom, the theater opened again after being closed for almost four decades. The art deco façade was painted a fresh bright pink; the white, pink, and red neon trim turned the building into a gleaming jewel on dark nights. Two movies were featured every three to four days, and it was a popular hangout for Saturday evening cruise-ins, where folks drove their vintage autos to town, and parked next to the theater for tailgating before the movie.

In 1970, Green Cove Springs was the setting for a wonderfully terrible, low budget B-rated horror film. *Zaat: The Blood Waters of Dr. Z* is the story of an embittered scientist determined to get revenge on his previous co-workers, the state of Florida, and the world, in that order. His plan involves transforming himself into a giant quasi-reptilian monster and creating an army of killer walking catfish to do his evil bidding. The laboratory in his basement is the headquarters for most of his schemes. There are all kinds of equipment with dials and meters and flashing lights, some resembling modified washing machines. There is a huge death chart on the wall, where the monster keeps track of his victims by checking them off with a ballpoint pen, and in the center of the room is a large tank of water.

The movie still has a cult following and gets featured a lot on bad horror movie websites. One reviewer describes the monster as a "demon born of an aardvark and spinach."

After his metamorphosis, the hulking, green, part-furry and part-scaly creature gets to work, squirting a toxic radioactive cocktail from a small plastic spray bottle along the riverbank, conveniently within walking distance of his house. When he is not contaminating the waterways of Florida with his spray bottle, he busies himself with murdering his old colleagues and spying on beautiful young women in bikinis, also all within walking distance. Much of the movie follows the reptile monster as he paces stiffly, laboriously around the town, peeking in windows, slashing people to death on their porches, and going surprisingly unnoticed in broad daylight.

During the filming in Green Cove Springs, townspeople were recruited as extras for non-speaking parts. Nina McKenzie, the organist at the local Methodist Church, jumped at the chance to appear. Her scene lasts for about eight seconds, where she clutches her white handbag to her bosom, an appropriately horrified look on her face. I am sorry Nina did not have a bigger role. Her flair for the dramatic would have added much-needed depth and authenticity to the film. Nonetheless, *Zaat* is solidly established in cult-classic horrible-horror-movie posterity.

After the old theater was restored and reopened, the owners announced they would bring *Zaat* back to Green Cove Springs for a special showing. I stopped by the theater late one afternoon to buy my ticket. The owner's son was there; he was slender, probably mid-30s, slick dark hair, sunken features and tattoos up both arms. He wore a heavy gold chain with a large gold cross around his neck.

"I am so excited that you are bringing *Zaat* back to Green Cove!" I told him. "I grew up here, and it's great to see the theatre open again."

We chatted about the theatre. I told him about my mother coming there to watch movies over seventy years ago.

"Do you know about the clock?" he asked me, gesturing above our heads.

I didn't, so he proceeded to tell me the story. Centered above the neon-lit marquee is a large octagonal clock. Its face is black during the day, the hands and numbers white. After dark, it reverses colors; the face turns white, and the hands and numbers turn black.

"We don't know why it does that." He took a drag on his cigarette and continued, "My dad hired a man from Ocala who came up here and got the clock working again, but he wouldn't tell us how it changes colors." The clock was a chameleon of sorts, another Floridian reptile.

I met a group of my friends at the theater on the night of the re-premier. It was a pleasantly warm evening in early December. The sky was darkening, and sure enough, the face of the clock was white. A small crowd congregated on the sidewalk.

The *Zaat* costume had been pulled out of storage from someone's basement in Jacksonville and loaned to the theater for the special showing. The seven-foot green figure stood on a small square of plywood, mounted on a dolly that had been wheeled to the front of the theatre entrance. He towered above the crowd, illuminated by makeshift floodlights set up on the sidewalk. A paper sign hung around his neck with a piece of string, giving him the appearance of a naughty schoolchild who has been caught misbehaving. The sign read: *Do Not Touch The Monster.* A light green leaf-bug landed on the empty head and gingerly crept around on the green fur. We took turns snapping pictures of ourselves in groups next to the monster, his bulging blue plastic eyes vacant and unseeing.

The theater was full that night, the atmosphere festive. Before the movie started, the director and a couple of the actors from the movie walked onstage and addressed the audience in front of the red velvet curtain. They made a special trip to Green Cove for this screening and were noticeably proud of the film, happy to see the turnout and show of support.

The camaraderie in the theater was palpable; the audience laughed aloud at the ridiculous scenes, unrealistic set-ups, corny plot devices. When the camera panned by the old Mayhugh's Drug Store sign, we cheered and clapped for the simple pleasure of seeing a beloved and long-gone landmark on the big screen. A favorite cameo appearance in the movie was by a local man, Shorty Garrett. Shorty was known in Green Cove as the guy with no front teeth who rode his bike around town wearing a big floppy brimmed hat, and whose home was a ramshackle box constructed from discarded pieces of wood and metal signs, hidden in the woods next to the river.

Back in the 1950s, a couple of men in town managed to get Shorty on the ballot for Constable. In an interview with the local newspaper, he didn't seem to have much of a platform, but indicated that he was a Goldwater man and had little use for President Johnson. Shorty originally had moved to Green Cove Springs with Barnum & Bailey's circus and was quoted in the article as saying, "I can make an elephant from anywhere do just about anything." While Shorty didn't win the election, he garnered a few votes and a memorable spot in the town's history.

When he wasn't pushing his bike around town collecting glass bottles or shining shoes at the barbershop, Shorty spent his days in the theatre, sitting on the front row, yelling and cursing at the screen. Kids who made too much noise behind Shorty were promptly admonished, "Boys, settle down or I'll snatch a knot in your tail!"

In a climactic scene of *Zaat*, a frantic crowd has gathered after dark on Walnut Street, and the Sheriff hops up onto the hood of a car to address the town, pleading for calm through his bullhorn. Shorty can be seen darting around the car wearing a new set of clothes that had been purchased for him by some sympathetic ladies in the community. It's said that he wore that outfit every day for the rest of his life.

In the last scene, the monster kidnaps a young female scientist and attempts to transform her into a sea-monster like himself, strapping her into a helicopter rescue basket and submerging her into the tank of electro-charged chemicals in his laboratory. The authorities are hot on his trail, so he abandons the lab and the submerged woman, escapes to the beach, slogs through the waves in his heavy green fur, and dives head first into the crashing waves. Suddenly, the woman appears on the beach in her ruffled white maxi-dress, stumbling along as if in a trance, staring at the ocean. She walks directly into the surf where the monster has just gone under. The two of them disappear into the ocean, never to be seen again, because there was no sequel to *Zaat*. Thank goodness.

The only thing missing from the re-premier of *Zaat* was Shorty Garrett. If Shorty were still alive, I know he would have been there that night, sitting on the front row, wearing a new suit that someone bought him. And if the crowd got too rowdy, he would turn around and snarl at us, "Y'all better shut the hell up!"

THIRTEEN

There are a number of secret organizations, a splendid newspaper, express telephone and telegraph offices, daily mails, county buildings, amusement halls, etc., too numerous to speak of in our limited space.

THE POCKET DIRECTORY OF GREEN COVE SPRINGS, 1889

ON THE OUTSIDE BACK wall of the pool hall, facing the cracked asphalt parking lot and a brown dumpster, is a mural of an oversized pool table. One-dimensional balls are scattered over a green rectangle. A cue stick lies across its surface; the game is paused, frozen in time. A line of rusted gutters frames the top of the mural; mildew and weeds creep up from below.

My friend Marilyn stayed in town after high school, married and divorced a few times. She's been playing competitive pool for twenty years. During my visits back, I realized my best chance for hanging out with her was to go to the pool hall on her league nights.

Sometimes my mother recalled that her father was a pool shark. "He played all the time, won lots of money," she said. "But he was a gambler and he took his winnings to the dog track and always lost it." Other times, Mom says he stayed for hours on end at the local pool hall but he didn't play. "Dad never had an education, and didn't really learn to read. He could sign his name, and that's about all." She shook her head, tisk-tisking to herself. "Don't you have to be able to write and keep score to play pool? I know my dad never could have done that. He just watched the other men play."

In my grandfather's day, the pool hall was located in one of the brick-front buildings along Walnut Street. Mom recalls being sent by her mother to fetch him home.

"There was a narrow alleyway between the buildings, and that's where the men went to relieve themselves. On a hot day, *phewww*! It would stink! They drank beer all day, and they'd pee in the alley." Her face would pinch up, recalling the bitter tangy smell of urine on hot Florida afternoons. "I had to stand outside and ask for him at the door. The men wouldn't allow any girls or women in the place."

Now the pool hall is in a squat cinderblock structure, a few blocks from the original pool hall of my mother's memory. Multi-colored Christmas icicle lights hang along the front year-round, both sides of the street usually lined with pickup trucks every night.

The first time I went to the pool hall, I sat on the sidelines, awkward and self-conscious, sipping a beer. There were men in greasy, sweat-stained t-shirts, muddied work boots, faded jeans. A young couple with lots of tattoos and wearing matching camo pants shot a game together. Players all around the room scanned the tables, smoking cigarettes, calculating, drinking beer, and working little blue chalk cubes back and forth on the ends of their cue sticks.

They were like military commanders on a battlefield, carefully considering every strategic move. I overheard bits and pieces of a language foreign to me: lagging for the break, top English, sandbagging, getting a good leave.

Marilyn is tall and slim; she wears her blonde hair in a short bob that frames her angular face. She took a few practice shots on an empty table before her match. Her face was set; she circled the table with brisk steps and her gaze never left the green felt.

On my first night there, Marilyn's opponent was an older woman, probably around sixty-five. Pam's gray hair reaches her waist. She wore a short floral sundress, spaghetti straps tied in bows on her shoulders. Her skin is dark, her mouth drawn down in a pouty frown. Her fingers were slim, and the tips of her fingernails were painted in crescents of bright red. Throughout the match, she moved slowly, circling the table with very little movement. In between plays, she smoked thin brown cigarettes. The third game in, Marilyn broke, dropped a solid ball, and continued to shoot. She followed the solids around the table, sank them all, putting the eight ball away last. The score keeper called out, "Hey Marilyn! Break and run! You got a break and run!" She had pocketed all of the balls without allowing her opponent a shot, and was so focused that she didn't realize what she had done. Pam walked around the table, gave her a hug and congratulated her.

Marilyn came over to hug me, a wide grin on her face. "That's my first-ever break and run! You've got to come back every Monday and be my mojo!"

After that, Mondays became my pool night, too. I hired a sitter for Mom on Monday nights, headed out the door around seven, and reminded her where I was going. Before I left, she always asked, "Do they allow women in the pool hall now?"

Marilyn sat next to me on a barstool between her matches and filled me in on the regulars. Freddie's gray hair hung to his shoulders. His t-shirt proclaimed *I got mine at Harley Heaven.* Amanda was tall with long black hair, a colorful tattoo sleeve on her left arm.

Chad was a senior in high school, at the pool hall every night. He was slim, blonde, with buzz-cut haircut and an attractive angular face; he wore military-style high-top black boots and shorts. His t-shirts had images of skulls and knives. He paced between the tables with a young athlete's grace, an intent look on his face, sipping an Orange Crush. Some weeks, he talked about going to junior college, other times about joining the Army. Chad flirted with Marilyn, whose own son is almost twice Chad's age. She flirted back, calling him "Baby."

Larry walked in the rear door late one Monday evening. He's Marilyn's ex, the one who taught her to play pool. He's tall, with a shaved head and graying short beard. Larry slowly worked the entire room, greeting everyone, chatting, sipping a long neck. Marilyn went to the jukebox, put some bills in, and James Taylor's *Steamroller* cranked up from the speakers. He finally made his way around to us; he and Marilyn embraced, sharing a laugh.

"I always like to play that song for him," she said later, grinning slyly.

After a few visits, Marilyn handed me a stick. "C'mon, I'm gonna teach you to play." I felt ridiculous; I didn't even know how to hold the stick properly. Marilyn set up some shots for me and explained the ghost ball idea.

"You were good in geometry in high school—you'll be good at this!" she said. "Imagine a ball is sitting exactly at the point of contact with the object ball. That's your ghost ball. Just make your cue ball go there."

Larry came over during my lessons. He watched my stroke, pointed out that my stance was too narrow, throwing off the angle of the tip. I corrected my stance, and the ball miraculously went where I wanted it to go, almost every time.

When Larry played, he was emotionless. His face was quiet; his eyes scanned the table; he chose his shot and rarely missed. "When I was young, I would see lines all over the table," he recalled. "It's something in my brain; I can't explain it. I can hit eight-on-the-breaks over and over." He took a swig from his bottle and kept talking. "It's a system for me, I guess; I see where all of the balls are going to end up, depending on where I hit on the break. I'd go out to Ethel's Roadhouse when I was still in high school, and the older guys would pay me a dollar for every eight-on-the-break I could make."

One night I was practicing alone on a table, killing time while Marilyn finished her match. I studied the angle to the pocket on a five-ball. Chad, the high-schooler, passed behind me, hesitated, pointed across the table, and said off-handedly, "Bank it there. Top-left English. Hit it solid." He took a drag from his cigarette and walked on to his table without looking back to see if I made the shot. I did.

On New Year's Eve, Marilyn and I met up with some friends for dinner at a Japanese steakhouse in the next town over. We finished up by nine o'clock, done with the chef's trite jokes, steaming rice-volcanoes, and flying shrimp tricks. Everyone else was heading home. We sat in the parking lot in Marilyn's car, and pondered our options. There weren't many.

"What about going to the pool hall?" I asked.

"Really?" Marilyn couldn't hide her surprise. "*You* want to go to the pool hall?" She laughed out loud. "I love it!" So she pulled out of the steakhouse parking lot and we drove back to Green Cove. The streets were empty and quiet. You would never know that it was a night for parties and reveling. But when we walked into the pool hall, the jukebox was blaring, there was a good-sized crowd, some of the regulars were playing at tables around the room. At midnight everyone gathered at the bar, and we rang in the New Year watching the ball in Times Square drop on the flat screen TV overhead. I kissed Marilyn and hugged strangers who reeked of cigarettes and booze.

After New Year's, Marilyn gave me one of her pool cues, the first one she owned. "Buy a case for it when you get back home. You don't want it banging around in your car." It was a Lucasi Hybrid, bird's-eye maple, stained a beautiful scarlet-black. Online, a new Lucasi ran about $400, an amount I would never spend for something like this. I liked the name because it sounded like an Italian sports car or a gangster's sub-machine gun.

Back in North Carolina, I checked out the pool halls around town and paid the annual membership fee to join one near my home. Ladies played free on Thursdays, so there I was most Thursdays when I wasn't in Florida, practicing on a table alone. "I'm packing my Lucasi," I'd say to myself when I walked in. I needed all the confidence I could muster.

After a couple of visits, the bartender recognized me. He knew I liked table number fifteen, so he would automatically book it when he saw me walk in. All he asked was whether I was drinking beer or bottled water. This was a decent pool hall—entrance was by key-card only, there was a posted dress code, and no smoking allowed. I got there around five o'clock. Usually I was the only one shooting pool, in a mostly-dark room of empty tables. ESPN played on the screens around the room, no one watching. Sometimes I hit drills, hitting cut balls over and over, working on angles. Other times, I practiced breaking. I was terrible at breaking. I would hit the cue ball as hard as I could toward the triangle of colored balls in the center of the table. Usually the best I got was a couple of the balls on the outside edge of the triangle dribbling away a few inches.

Table fifteen was in the back corner of the room, the farthest from the bar and the jukebox. I didn't want anyone seeing me practice. Marilyn's voice buzzed in my brain. "Hold your stance steady, keep your legs this far apart and flexible. Don't over-grip the end of the stick; hold it loosely. Your elbow—keep it at a right angle. Easy, stroke through it. Stroke, don't poke. Remember that. Stroke, don't poke, it's important."

"Make sure you're hitting the dead center of the cue ball. We'll worry about English later. Dead center. Do you have the ghost ball visualized? You just want your cue ball to be where that ghost ball was."

"Watch the object ball when you strike. Don't pull up after you've hit. Stay down until your cue ball has stopped moving. Put your chin right there on the stick. Get down low with it. That way you can see that you have everything lined up. OK, stroke it—easy!"

I never knew my mother's father. I'm not even sure what he looked like, but I have thought about him a lot since I started playing pool. Did he really play pool, or did he just sit on the side and watch the other men? Did he have his own cue stick? If he played, was he good? Could he see the angles like Larry does?

Another trip to Florida, I was sitting with Marilyn at the bar. She just won in eight-ball against a man she had never beaten before. She was keyed up.

"Guys think there's something sexy about hitting bottom English. What is that about? Seeing how hard you can spin the cue ball back to yourself. Why do they always want to do that?"

Marilyn tamped out her cigarette butt in the plastic ashtray. She was not a regular smoker, but carried two or three cigarettes in her purse on league nights. She would light up if she were having a tough game.

Jake and Chad played on the table in front of us. Jake's dark curly hair was a tangled mass. He had a bushy beard and wore a faded t-shirt from a bar in Daytona Beach. He didn't have a lot of finesse; he smacked the hell out of the cue ball every time. Still, with no control but pretty good aim, he pocketed a fair number of balls. He was also scratching frequently, so Chad had ball in hand several times.

Chad's game was smooth, fluid, effortless. He rarely stopped to study a shot. "He doesn't think defensively. He shoots without thinking about his next shot every time. I've tried to tell him, but he won't listen to me. He won't take criticism from a female," Marilyn commented, holding her green Beck's bottle close to her lips.

According to Marilyn, Mike was the best player in the house. He sat at the bar wearing a faded Hawaiian-print shirt, watching the tables and rolling cigarettes from generic tobacco in a blue foil pouch.

"This is the cheap stuff," he explained. "I can get about three days off one of these bags. That's less than two bucks." Mike smokes non-stop.

"Yeah, chances are I got lung cancer. So whaddya do? I figure I can buy myself a new set of lungs for eighty-grand." He cackled loudly at his own joke. When he got off the barstool to play, he talked to himself, chuckling, shaking his head, muttering a running commentary on the other games in the room.

I sat with Mike one evening, and he tried to teach me how to keep the league scorecards. He had a talent for watching multiple games at one time, keeping up with each one, noting the difficult shots, even several tables away. I didn't do so well with the scorecards.

"That's outrageous! D'ya see that over there?" Mike pointed across the room. "Chad's leading Larry but only by a hair. He better watch this next shot. Better keep his speed down. You know those young guys—they gotta show off their stuff."

Mike wandered over to get another beer, chatted with a few people, leaving the scorecard on the table. When he returned, the game he was scoring had ended.

"Hey, is it over? Who won? Ah, hell, nobody will care about this shit by closing time anyway." He sat down, laughing, and rolled another cigarette.

One night, Chad was showing off his first tattoo. It was in a delicate Gothic script, two inches high, and ran the length of his inner arm from elbow to wrist. *RUCKSICHTLUS.* The lettering was lovely; I asked him about it.

"It's German for reckless," he explained. "My grandmother spoke German, and so does my father." He had a slight grin on his face as he points out the last letter closest to the inner elbow. "That one bled the most."

He packed up his cue stick to leave early. "Yeah, it's fucking Senior Slave Day at school tomorrow. I gotta go buy a goddamned pink shirt to wear," he smirked, slinging his cue bag over one shoulder, heading out the back door to the parking lot. Later, I looked up the odd German word. The Internet tells me that Rücksichtslos means ruthless, not reckless, and it's not spelled the way Chad's tattoo artist spelled it. But it didn't matter—it sure was a beautiful tattoo.

Richard was a regular, came in after work from St. Augustine. After I had been to the pool hall a few times, he struck up a conversation and bought me a beer. He was married, but his wife didn't come to the pool hall.

"She's been here a couple of times, but she doesn't like it," he explained. Richard always asked when I am coming back to town. "Play pool with me next time, promise?" I would put him off, since I had a fear of a jealous wife who might have access to something with more firepower than my Lucasi.

One evening I sat in my car in the parking lot behind the pool hall, studying the lie of the balls on the mural. The solids were stacked nicely on one end of the table. It was more than a flat, unimaginative painting. It was a potential game, a challenge. I saw that if I put correct English on the cue ball, I would be in a good position to run five balls on this table. The yellow one-ball was easy; after that, the three and the six were lined up to make a nice combo shot. The four-ball was problematic, surrounded by stripes, but maybe a hard bank shot to the right corner...?

After I had been playing a few months, Marilyn put together a Scotch Doubles match, pairing me with Mike, and she partnered with Freddie. Mike's gravelly voice replaced Marilyn's in my head.

"Partner, hit the center of the cue ball. Hit it slow. You'll be able to see your mistakes. You have to back up the cue stick slow, too. Follow-through keeps the stick steady. The speed of the follow-through needs to match your pull-back."

Although I'm a heavy handicap, Mike and I managed to lead the match; on one play, Freddie took a defensive shot and set the leave strategically. It was my turn, and I didn't see a play. Freddie turned from the table, forcing a high-five from Marilyn.

Mike pulled me aside. "They've left us a shitty table, partner." He studied the table for a moment, then put his arm over my shoulder.

"OK, all you got to do is hit it light. Don't worry. Just tap the ball and leave the cue ball down to the right. We don't need to pocket the ball. Just get it in the neighborhood. If you can place it just right, then they won't have a shot. It's always better to be lucky than good, partner. Always better to be lucky than good."

I set my aim, stroked, and the object ball swung in a slow angle to the right, skirted behind the ball Freddie had left, and miraculously pocketed in the corner.

Mike grinned, astonished; Marilyn let out a happy whoop. Damn, that felt good.

Later, I pulled up into my mother's driveway. The living room window was full of light, casting a yellow rectangle on the grass in the dark yard. I let myself in the front door. Mom was asleep on the sofa, but woke up when I walked in. My hair, my clothes, even my skin reeked of cigarette smoke. She followed me through the kitchen to the darkened back porch. As I peeled off my clothes next to the washing machine and left them in a heap on the floor to be washed tomorrow, she asked me again, "Do they allow women in the pool hall now?"

FOURTEEN

The delightful two hours spent in reaching Green Cove Springs, like a dream has passed, and where the grand old river makes its most majestic sweep—miles in width— the traveler gets his first glimpse of Green Cove Springs, the finest located town on the river.

THE POCKET DIRECTORY OF GREEN COVE SPRINGS, 1889

IN THE LATE 1800s, when Green Cove Springs was a bustling tourist destination, the majority of visitors arrived by boat. Steamers and paddleboats would dock at the city pier. An archway on the pier welcomed visitors. But it must have been a project overseen by a committee, because as passengers disembarked from their vessels, they were greeted by a sign that read "Green Cove Springs – Read the Other Side." On the back side of the sign, the side that they would naturally see as they departed Green Cove Springs and headed to their boat to go back home, read "We Welcome You to Green Cove Springs."

X X

One summer evening after supper I walked to the pier. The sky and water were illuminated by light and clouds. The bench at the end of the pier was empty, so I sat. I had only been there a few minutes when a woman approached. I had seen her at other times on the pier, walking alone late in the day, drinking from a red Solo cup. She wore a medical scrubs top peppered with words in lime green and pink and purple: Happiness. Charity. Love. Kindness.

"It's a nice evening," she offered as she sat down next to me. Her words slurred. She spoke as if she had wet cotton in her mouth. "So what do you do? Do you work?"

"Yes, I have a job and I'm a writer."

She squinted her eyes at me. "Oh, a writer! You want somebody to pay you for that bullshit, don't you?" Before I could think of a response to that, she asked, "Are you married?"

I hesitated, then replied, "I'm widowed."

"Aren't you blessed!" she exclaimed, then she mumbled on about men, money, life insurance. "The man I'm married to now is always worried about money, but that didn't stop him from buying a Mercedes. All he cares about is money." She frowned. "He says, 'Oh, you're just waiting for me to die so you can have the Mercedes.'"

She continued rambling. Divorces, stepchildren, retirement, money. "We're on Social Security, we got no globe-trotter money." Then she leaned in closer to me and half-whispered, "I'm going to bury him in that damned Mercedes."

X X

A mud-splattered pickup truck is parked at the pier. Massive lug-tread tires, darkened windows, hunting decals

on the back window, and this bumper sticker: *Don't laugh.*
Your daughter may be in here.

X X

Another evening, another stroll to the pier. A couple
was seated about halfway out. As I got closer, I realized they
had a hookah set up next to their folding chairs. The man
was fishing from the side of the pier, casting, reeling in. He
had dark hair and a mustache, wore a faded blue Florida
Lottery t-shirt. The woman tended to the hookah. I'd never
seen a hookah in person, so I stopped to chat.

The woman smiled, pulled a small round tin of tobacco
from a cloth bag, showed me how it works. "We like the
hookah because the tobacco is not as strong. The water
makes it milder."

She looked to be about thirty-five, petite, with dark, kind
eyes, her brown hair in a braid that hung down her back.
"We came from Syria. We've lived here four years. My
husband does not speak English, but he has a good job in a
warehouse in Jacksonville." Her husband, focused on his
fishing, kept his back to us while we talked.

She showed me how the hookah works, the base, the
tube, the small shallow bowl lined with aluminum foil. "It is
good that I only set it up once a week, because it is a lot of
trouble."

I thanked her for showing it to me and walked on,
leaving her to tend the hookah, her husband to his fishing.

X X

As I walked out onto the pier late one morning, there was an elderly man sitting on a bench reading a book, his metal frame walker parked next to him. He was dressed very neatly, wearing khaki pants, red plaid shirt, and had a closely trimmed mustache. The title of the book was "Why Women Should Rule the World."

"How's the book?" I asked.

"It's pretty good, but I'm not sure I'm convinced," he admitted. He told me that he was 89 years old, and he tries to keep an open mind about everything. I walked away feeling encouraged.

X X

A man was walking with slow careful steps along the sidewalk toward the pier one evening. There was a gray object on his shoulder, making noises. A squirrel? When I got closer, I realized it's an African gray parrot, and they are bantering back and forth. The parrot dipped his head mechanically. The man grinned as I pass.

X X

I stood on the footbridge that crosses the spring run before it merges with the wide St. Johns River. Dark green grasses shifted with the flowing current beneath the bridge. A box turtle had pulled himself out of the water and sat, covered in black muck, on the bank next to the bridge. A man on a bicycle slowly approached the bridge. He was maybe 70, short-cut white hair and a long white Fu Manchu mustache. His skin was tanned and weathered; he was wearing a sleeveless undershirt and olive-green cargo pants. A black plastic trash bag covered the contents of the basket on the front of his bike, secured with a bungee cord. A half-empty plastic Gatorade bottle was wedged into the side of the basket.

"Did ya see that turtle there?" he stopped his bike on the bridge to chat.

"Yeah, I did!" I pointed down stream to another dark lump next to the water. "There's another one."

"I can't believe the gators don't come up here in this spring! They're out there in the river." I noticed a diamond stud earring in his left earlobe. "We seen a head come up out of the water," he held his hands apart two feet, "probably this big. I bet that gator was ten feet long."

He went on. "My buddy was out swimming off the pier the other night, and a gator got ahold of his leg! Right below the knee—you can see the teeth marks. He wasn't hurt bad; it wasn't nothing. Probably a little gator." He chuckled. "And he's talking about going back in! I told him he's crazy." The man pointed at the swimming pool. "If I'm going swimming, that's where I'll go." He pushed off on his bike and started toward the pier. "Have a good one," he called over his shoulder.

X X

A friend of mine was getting her hair cut in a local salon. I sat in the waiting area, thumbing through a magazine. There were random items for sale on a shelf: bagged pecans for a local church fundraiser, beaded necklaces, aprons, hair clips embellished with ribbons made by customers. One of the beauticians walked around the shop, pouring Barefoot brand Pinot Grigio from Walgreens in clear plastic cups for all of us. This was the third hair-styling establishment I'd visited in town where serving alcohol throughout the day is the norm.

The beautician was probably sixty-something, wore a low-cut, skin-tight lace top, purple leggings, tattoos above her breasts and on her upper arms, bleached-blonde hair piled up in a loose knot on the top of her head.

After serving the wine, she returned to the woman waiting in her chair. "Do you want wine, Denise?"

"No, I don't care for wine. I'll just take a Sprite. Do you have Sprite?"

"Let me go look. We don't have a drink machine." The beautician walked through a curtain to a back room, emerged a few seconds later. "No, I'm out of Sprite. I'll go get you one."

She then walked out of the shop, across the street and up the block to a gas station, returning a few minutes later with a cold Sprite for her customer.

X X

There have always been men who ride rusty old bikes around Green Cove Springs. When I was a kid, one of the men was the movie-extra and almost-Constable Shorty Garrett, pushing his bike by the handlebars and collecting empty Coke bottles in his basket. Another old wizened man sold bacon and eggs, going door to door on his bike. These days the bikes are mostly loaded with fishing gear, bags holding gathered aluminum cans, or lightered knots for sale, toted in a cart behind the bike.

One of these guys approached me in the pool hall as I was getting a beer at the bar. Grizzled stubble covered his chin; he had kind blue eyes and bad teeth. He grinned, assuming a familiarity between us, even though we had never met.

"I hit an eight-on-the-break on the quarter table" he beamed.

"Well, that's great! This might be a good day for you to go buy a lottery ticket," I reply. It sounded snarky, but I was happy for him, and just couldn't think of anything else to say.

His face lit up and he laughed. "Hey! That's a good idea! I think I'll do that!"

On another day, I was in McDonald's, getting a sausage biscuit for Mom. It was early, and a group of retired men who meet for coffee every morning had already claimed their booth. Several of them wore military service hats. Navy, Marines, World War II, Korea, Vietnam. One of the local bike-riders pulled up. He leaned his bike against an old oak tree next to the parking lot, walked inside, and got in line. It was a chilly morning. He was tall, wore a ragged coat, scuffed work boots, dirty jeans.

Outside, a small elderly man wearing a Navy hat limped, hunched over, toward the entrance. Bike-rider guy saw him, left the line, and walked quickly to the door. He opened it and picked up the elderly man like a sack of potatoes across his chest. He elbowed the door open, brought the man inside, and set him down. As the old man slowly made his way to the booth and his friends, bike-rider guy said, "I would've come and got you at your car. Next time let me know."

X X

In the 1960s and 70s, Green Cove Springs had car dealerships from all of the major American car manufacturers. Ford, Chrysler, Buick, Chevrolet, Dodge, there was a dealership on every corner. "Take a drive to Little Detroit," the ads on the Jacksonville TV stations proclaimed. The dealerships would leave the ignition keys in the cars on the lots, and for a while, cars started disappearing. It was a mystery. No dealership in particular was targeted, and only one car would go missing at a time. Eventually it was discovered that a young man in town was taking the cars for a spin, driving them out west of town to an empty field. There, he'd sit in the car and listen to the radio until the battery died, then he'd walk back to town and get another car.

X X

A Green Cove friend emailed me. Several of her goats had died, and more were sick.

"We don't know why they are dying, so we're going to put one on ice and take him to the state vet lab in Lake City. Husband runs up the road to get ice at the gas station, with a dead goat in the back of the truck, and the bank freezes his card. Fraud alert five miles from home, trying to spend $20 on gas and ice. Vet said it's possible someone's poisoning them, so we had a massive goat evacuation to an undisclosed location last night. They'll stay there until necropsy results are in. Dead goat handed off to daughter for the ride to the lab."

A few hours later, a goat update email:

"Daughter was turned away. Said they don't accept large animals and she needs to take it to the other state lab in Kissimmee. She tried to convince them it's just a miniature goat, but no deal."

"We have put all of the surviving goats into the witness protection program and are assigning aliases for them. The jet black goat will have to be Whitey now. Plum Pretty becomes Plain Ugly. Kansas (she was born during a tornado) will be Hawaii. Kero Satos (some kind of Japanese candy that I've never heard of and am probably misspelling) will be Nerds. I'm changing Tequila Sunrise to my favorite drink, Malibu and Pineapple. And finally, Lunchbox will become Snack Pack. I'll have to check and see who is still alive, to see if I need to come up with more names."

Another goat update email:

"Just got word - daughter broke down on Interstate 75 south of Ocala with the dead goat, a live dog, and melting ice. We are heading down there now with our truck and back-up ice."

Next goat update email:

"We had to stop twice for ice as because it is so hot outside. When I stopped the truck quickly in traffic for the first time, the tub moved up towards the front of the cab and then a wall of water and ice went over the top of us! We were waiting for the poor dead goat in a bag to go sliding over the windshield too! Didn't happen and we got there finally. Toll worker at the tollbooth outside Orlando asked what was in the container in the back, and didn't believe us. I bet she will not ask anyone else what they have in the back of their truck. Afterwards we went to a great bistro. Had mimosas and toasted the goats. Well, you know what I mean. Got back to Green Cove about 10:00 that night."

Goat dénouement: It was determined the goats had become resistant to their deworming medicine. Meds adjusted, no more dead goats on ice transported across the state by this family. At least, not that I've heard.

X X

Even my monster illuminated street pageant in New York, which will draw many persons a hundred miles from home to witness it and which I would not miss seeing for a considerable sum, is not sufficiently powerful to draw me from this most charming and delightful winter retreat. If not telegraphed for, I shall remain at least another fortnight in this salubrious and almost enchanted health-restoring spot. I mail you a pamphlet setting forth some of its good qualities. Suffice it that they are sufficient to induce me to build a winter cottage here. I am determined to be as wise as the birds in choosing a winter's climate, not hot, but which renders the impure air from furnaces unnecessary, and also enables us to sit in the open air and walk, ride and sail through the most invigorating and delightful atmosphere I have ever found.

~ P.T. Barnum, 1881

FIFTEEN

MY MOTHER NEEDED an eye exam, so I took her to the optical shop in town, an old house on Highway 17. I was surprised to find a wide selection of the latest designer frames—Oakley, Coach, Via Spiga—as well as a side room that housed a sort of girly-boutique—bejeweled flip-flops, flashy rings, tote bags and purses in neon pink zebra prints. Not the kind of merchandise normally found in Green Cove Springs. Then I noticed something odd. Interspersed between the trendy eyeglass frames and Juicy Couture scarves were belts and knife sheaths made of snakeskin. Real snakeskin. Reptilian brocades in shades of muted grays and browns, lying flat on the top shelf of the glass display case. There was something sinister about all of that snakeskin among the pink and sequins and fluff. When I asked Kendall, the owner, about the snakeskin pieces, she replied proudly, "Those are made by my husband, Hoofer."

I have never understood the aesthetic appeal of snakeskin, so of course I had to interview this guy. Shoot, the fact that his name was Hoofer was enough to make me want to meet him. I didn't know what to expect, but I can say what I hoped for: a grizzled old guy, salty, gruff. In this, I was disappointed.

It was a muggy morning when I drove north on Highway 17 to visit Hoofer. Turning west on the old dairy road, I ended up in a deserted cul-de-sac, overgrown by tall weeds, faded real estate signs marking off the empty lots. I looped around the paved circle and returned, this time looking more carefully for a dirt driveway after the last curve in the road. The house was on the left; on the right was a tall shed with an old metal fishing boat parked underneath.

Hoofer came out from behind the shed. A slim man in his early 60s with short gray hair and a trim beard, he wore a t-shirt, denim shorts and Teva flip-flops. He looked more like an aging surfer than a backwoods snake skinner.

Greeting me with a friendly but shy smile, he seemed genuinely pleased that I had come out to see his work. I followed him into his workshop, a small air-conditioned room adjacent to the boat shed. The workbench inside was tidy, with a couple of vise grips, hoses, a green cutting mat with one-inch grid marks, just like the ones I use when I sew. A diamondback rattler's skin was mounted on one wall, over six feet long. It's the biggest one he's ever killed.

"I don't kill snakes for their skins. I kill them if they are in my yard, you know, if they're big and I don't want them around. People bring them to me if they run over them in the road."

Hoofer reached up on a long shelf and pulled down a stack of flat, stiff snakeskins. Four, five, six feet long, and anywhere from three to eight inches wide. They were like thin pieces of tree bark. Grays and browns, speckled with deeper browns and blacks, repeating hypnotic geometric patterns. All similar, but with unique differences, like snowflakes. Earth-toned tessellations.

The differences in the various species are what draw Hoofer in. He favors timber rattlers and corn snakes, with their strong, distinct markings. Water moccasins have subtle brown designs.

"This one was in the shade a lot." He pulled out a pale glistening gray skin; the pattern barely visible. "It's a rattler. Probably lived in captivity, like in a box at a nature center. You see how there's not much color? When they are light like that, they haven't had much exposure to the sun." He ran his hand down the scales. "They are just like us that way."

When someone brings him a snake, he strips out the insides, and freezes the skins until he is ready to cure them. A chest freezer sits under the shed just outside the door to his shop. He pulled open the freezer door. The cold blast felt good in the steamy morning air. Smaller snakes were in little plastic containers, like you would use for leftover lasagna. The bigger ones were coiled up in gallon zip bags. Stacked in orderly columns were frosty coiled rattlers, corn snakes, and a python, their patterns showing through the clear bags. The brilliant coppery-orange feathers of a rooster were curled and tucked in the middle of a stack of snakes. A gruesome three-toed turkey foot reached skyward from between two bags. It was like gazing into the icy pantry of a satanic chef.

He pulled out the bag that held the python and handed it to me. The snake inside was large, yellow and white. "Feel how heavy it is? That's just the skin. No guts."

When he has enough skins saved up, Hoofer pulls them out of the freezer and soaks them in five-gallon buckets of preserving solution hung shoulder-high on a rope line strung up in his shed. "I shake them whenever I walk by. They have to be agitated every now and then." He estimates that he puts about thirty hours into curing each skin.

Along with creating objects from snakeskins, Hoofer also makes beautiful knives with bone handles and tungsten steel blades. "I've always been crafty," he admits modestly. He reaches into a small box on his workbench full of alligator teeth, pulling out the biggest one. "I'm going to make Kendall a necklace out of this one."

We walked over to the house so he could show me a few more finished pieces. I immediately noticed a huge alligator head on top of the hutch in the dining room. "That gator came out of the river. He was an eleven footer."

A long strip of rattler skin was draped across the back of a kitchen chair. After the skins are soaked and dried outside, he cuts them into pieces and does the tedious job of lacing them together while watching TV in his den in the evenings. He creates belts, knife sheaths, cell phone holsters. "I don't make any money when I sell these things. It's very time-consuming, and my labor ends up being free."

Walking back across the yard toward my car, Hoofer interrupted our conversation to stop and shoo away a large black Persian cat. The cat scuttled into the shrubbery against the house.

"That cat has been after the baby birds all week. I think he's gotten almost all of them." He showed me the nest near the front door. We could see the head of one baby bird bobbing deep inside the darkness of the nest. "I hope that one can make it."

SIXTEEN

MARILYN AND I MET the year that we were in third grade together, but I have few memories of her in class with me that year, or on the playground, or in the lunchroom. Marilyn wasn't at school very much because she spent a lot of third grade in the hospital. On a sunny October afternoon after church, in the church parking lot with her family, a little boy picked up a dead armadillo and started chasing her. Marilyn ran as fast as she could away from him, directly into a car coming up the street.

Marilyn recalls being mortified the next year at my ninth birthday party, when her mother pulled up Marilyn's dress to show my mother the "roadmap to Tennessee" across her torso. Her tiny abdomen was crisscrossed with scar tissue—pink keloid lines from the surgical incisions.

In high school, Marilyn and I took turns spending Friday nights at each other's house. I lived in town, she lived west of the city limits where houses sat on large parcels of land, the acreage of Gustafson's dairy fenced off for miles along the road to her house. We would sit on her screened front porch in the swing, talking late into the night, mostly about boys. The next morning her mother would drive me back to town in her white Ford Fairlane. The windows rolled down, gospel music on the radio, a blur of pine trees whizzing by on both sides of the car, the road straight, flat, gray.

The day of Marilyn's mother's funeral, the skies were high and blue, no clouds yet, though they would come in later, towering, billowing stormheads that roll in every afternoon from the beaches twenty miles east of here. But early in the day, there were no textures, no bold structures in the skies. Only a high translucent blue skin.

I had driven down for the visitation and funeral, this time only staying for a long weekend with Mom. Just past town, deep groves of slash pine and scrub palmetto lined the road on both sides. I passed the Rehab Saloon on the right, then just ahead on the left was the drive for Mrs. Moody's church.

The church sat back off the highway behind an RV and boat storage yard. A man in a dark suit and purple tie, standing at the edge of the drive, waved me over. There was no parking lot; all the cars were parked on the sandy dirt under trees. I rolled down the window. He was smoking a cigarette and courteously held it away with an outstretched arm as he leaned toward my car.

"If you're going to the graveside service after the funeral, then pull to the right over yonder behind that car." He pointed with his cigarette hand.

After parking, I saw a couple of Marilyn's friends that I've met at the pool hall, standing in a group behind a black SUV with "Salt Life" and skull and crossbones decals. I stepped awkwardly in their direction, the heels of my black pumps sinking in the soft sand. As we entered the church, we were greeted with a banner in the foyer: *We are 110% Pentecostal!*

The ceiling was low, with commercial acoustic tile and florescent light fixtures. At the front of the sanctuary was a large brown wooden cross backlit with purple florescent lights, a Hammond organ, a drum set. Funeral sprays on spindly stands perched in front of the altar like long-legged exotic birds, full of lilies and pink carnations and white roses, angel-hair fern fronds and drooping satin ribbons. People filed in, some families with children, mostly older folks. There was no prelude music, just the hum of voices as people visited across the aisle and over pews. At eleven o'clock, a man's voice at the back of the church announced, "All, please rise."

The casket was slowly wheeled in by the pallbearers, followed by the minister and family. Marilyn and her father walked in together. Both are reed-thin and tall, long-limbed, with angular faces. She has always been her dad's daughter, no mistaking that. Marilyn's face was drawn, tired. She had her arm around her father's waist.

A quartet stood behind the altar: two women, a young teen-aged girl, and a man. One of the women was barefoot. Each held a microphone in their hands, and they sang.

When I come to the river at the ending of day
When the last winds of sorrow have blown
There'll be somebody waiting to show me the way
I won't have to cross Jordan alone.

The churches I attend, when I attend church, don't have drum sets and florescent crosses and microphones. The musicians are often paid professionals, always wearing shoes, and dressed in tasteful black outfits, tuxedoes and long skirts; they play expensive instruments—violins, oboes, cellos. I've heard my share of Bach and Widor and Handel in church services for the last thirty years. And I would pay money to hear this quartet sing again. Their voices were full and rich and earnest, blending in pitch-perfect harmony.

At the end of the song, the piano player stood; he was a young man, perspiring in his gray suit. He spoke earnestly about Mrs. Moody, how she was "Grandma" to the people in the congregation.

"There was a time in my life when I was facing many troubles." He alluded to unnamed struggles and temptations. "I had a protracted battle with the devil. But Grandma let me know every Sunday morning that she was praying for me."

He sat back down at the piano, and the minister stood behind the pulpit. He prayed and gestured, exhorting the congregation about salvation and repentance and eternal life. He recalled the last time that he shared a meal with Mrs. Moody and the family after church one Sunday, at Sam's St. Johns Seafood Restaurant. "No one loved crab legs like Grandma."

Mrs. Moody was a good cook, and sometimes when I spent the night, she made pan biscuits. They were unlike any other biscuit I've ever eaten. She baked them in a square pan instead of on a baking sheet. The biscuits sort of melded together, so that when they were baked and out of the oven, you had to cut them apart, like brownies. Their texture was delicate and crumbly, and they were so delicious. Marilyn admitted to me much later that the secret to those biscuits was lard.

The preacher had an altar call before the service ended. He gazed across the congregation. "If you grandchildren would come to the Lord on this day, your Grandma would be so proud. She is sitting in heaven now, looking down on you. Hoping you will turn your lives over to the Lord." The grandchildren sat fidgeting, but mute. Mrs. Moody sighed in heaven. No young lives were surrendered.

The last hymn, *My Name is Written in the Book*, was lively; people clapped and raised their hands. The congregation joined in the singing. When the music ended, we stood, filed out, walked to our cars, started the engines and the air conditioning. The ride to the cemetery took about 25 minutes. We rode slowly, bumper to bumper along County Road 209, skirting the western side of the old Shattalon Dairy.

Appropriately, ironically, *Free Bird* by Lynyrd Skynyrd came on the radio. The Van Zandt brothers held their earliest jam sessions in a barn less than three miles from here. There is a lot of local pride in claiming Lynyrd Skynyrd as our own. I turned off the air and dangled my arm out the car window in the sunshine. We inched along, next to grassy fields, crickets buzzing. The smell of cigarette smoke from the car behind me drifted into my open window.

Drivers of the cars coming from the opposite direction pulled over and waited on the shoulder of the road, in that lovely Southern gesture of respect for the funeral cortege. On the morning of my father's funeral, riding in the back seat of Charlie Helm's shiny black funeral home Cadillac, I looked out the window and saw a logging truck pulled over to the side of the road. The driver, a slim man, stood still on the road next to the cab of the truck, watching as we rode by, his soiled cap in his hand. I will never forget him.

The Moody plot is close to my father's grave in the Hickory Grove cemetery. From my place in the graveside crowd, I could see my father's name spelled out in gray granite just beyond Marilyn's parents' headstone. The day we buried my father was much like this one. Sunny, muggy, crows calling out from the tops of tall pines at the edge of the cemetery. The oppressive heat in the shade of the funeral home tent. A blanket of bright green indoor-outdoor carpet covering the mound of dirt just beyond the casket. People dressed up in Sunday clothes on a day that's not Sunday, then heading to their cars and returning to their lives.

After the final prayer, Marilyn and I linked arms and walked away from the gravesite.

"How'd you get your legs to look like that—tanned and sorta sparkly?" she asked.

"Sally Hansen spray-on legs," I replied. "Now that panty hose are out, I need to do something with my pale legs before I go out in public."

Marilyn threw her head back and laughed the same laugh I have loved for over fifty years. "I use that stuff, too!"

"When are you going to move back here, girl?" she asked. "We could use you on our pool team."

I smiled. "Yeah, that would be fun." I looked away, my eyes watering. The sun was bright.

As I walked from the gravesite, I thought about the road trip I would be taking in a few days. Back to North Carolina, past the moss-tree at Bowman and the Eastern Continental Moss Divide, back to rolling hills, cooler weather, civilization.

The hardest part of the return drive is when I pass the south Georgia tidewater area. I skim past the eastern fringes of the Great Okefenokee Swamp on a series of low, flat bridges. Driving north in the dawn, listening to the outer reaches of a Jacksonville radio station, notes from a country song, scratchy, fading. The boggy water is stippled with marsh grasses and cattails, its surface shimmers in the early-morning light. The water, the tree line in the distance, the low clouds, then the sky. Long horizontal layers, parallel striations of muted colors—pinks, blues, lavenders— blooming in the early morning sunlight, creating a horizon rainbow. Moss hangs from the cypress trees at the shoreline. After about an hour in the car, I take exit 36-A at Brunswick. That's my Starbucks, every trip. The caffeine eases the pain of my leaving.

SEVENTEEN

A FEW DAYS BEFORE my next trip to Florida I was filling my suitcase, making stacks on the guest bed, reviewing my list of items to pack. As I chatted on the phone one evening with a friend, she asked, "Have you thought about sewing with your mom?" Her grandmother had suffered with dementia for several years before her death. My friend knew well the agitation and emptiness that her grandmother had experienced as she slipped away from reality.

"Maybe you could take some fabric down there and get her sewing machine out. It might be something to interest her, distract her from her pain."

I thought this was a great idea, and since I have been sewing for a long time, I have enough scraps from years of sewing projects to fill a small barn. I gathered a big bag of bright, happy cottons, folds and cuts left over from several quilts I've pieced in the last few years, and crammed the bag into the trunk of the car.

Once I settled in with Mom, I dragged her sewing machine out of the back-bedroom closet and set it up on the round table in her small dining room. It's an aqua-colored Singer, circa 1967, and heavy as a horse. Like many girls in that era, I learned to sew from my mother years before taking home-ec classes at school.

Patiently she showed me how to cut from a pattern holding her big black and silver metal shears in my small hand, explaining the general principles of simple garment construction and how to operate the aqua-colored machine. I made little pincushions, a folding wallet, clothes for my Barbie dolls, red felt Christmas stockings embellished with sequins that I sold to neighbors. By the time I was around thirteen, I graduated to making some of my own clothes.

Mom's memory and experience of her own childhood and sewing machines were vastly different from mine. "When I was a little girl," she recalled, "my mother had a treadle machine, and she wouldn't let any of us near it. She fussed at us if we touched it."

I plopped the bag of scraps on a chair next to the china cabinet and put up the ironing board under the window. It had been forty years since I had sewn on this machine, and probably at least ten since my mother had used it. I found empty bobbins, wound several of them full of thread. Then I ran the top thread through all the little loops and guides, cut the thread to give it a fresh sharp end, squeezed it with a licked finger, and pushed the end through the needle's eye. I scooted a scrap under the presser foot and hit the gas. The machine didn't hesitate. It was off to the races, and so were we.

"That's my old sewing machine that your Dad bought me, isn't it?" Mom asked, sitting at my elbow.

"Yes! You sewed a lot of clothes for us on this machine, Mom. Do you remember that lavender maxi dress you made in the 70s?" The memory of my shy, careful mother in a hippie dress is still an inspiration to me. "I think you even wore it to church!" No, she didn't recall it.

I decided to start a quilt top that would be made from strips, so there would not be any complicated cutting or patterns to follow. Sure enough, Mom was easily drawn into this activity. There was color and motion, and a topic that she could understand and talk about.

"I don't sew anymore," she seemed apologetic. "My eyesight isn't what it used to be." She busied herself with the mound of scraps that spilled out of the bag. Drawing out piece after piece, she carefully folded them into flat squares.

With my rotary cutter and a couple of clear acrylic sewing rulers, I cut yards and yards of two-inch wide strips while Mom poked through the bag, folding odd-shaped pieces, repeating her questions and comments. Lemon yellows, oranges as bright as traffic cones, neon greens, brilliant reds, royal blues, rich purples, flaming pinks. Bright, happy, crazy color combinations that sang and danced against the oak tabletop.

"Your Dad bought that sewing machine for me, didn't he?"

We sat across from each other at the round dining room table, sometimes late into the evening. The sewing, ironing, and sorting colors seemed to ground her. She could sit for thirty, forty minutes, an hour, fully distracted by the colors, the process. Never once asking for pain meds. Most days this was the longest stretch of time that she would sit awake, still, and contented.

The sewing calmed me as well. It was a way to immerse myself in the beautiful fabrics, the steadiness of straight lines and measurements. Sometimes it felt like the only straight and steady thing that I had to hold on to. I loved the sweet smell of steam on cotton, the satisfying feel of a sharp blade cutting through fabric, the hum of this dear old machine from my childhood.

In those sewing times together, we were our old selves again. Enjoying a shared pastime, working together with a common purpose. After I cut a big stack of strips, I sliced them into six-inch lengths, and Mom would sort the rectangles by color. There was no way she would ever again be able to construct a garment, lay out a geometric quilt design, cut fabric with scissors or sew a simple straight line. But when we sat together, she didn't know that. We were making this quilt together.

I threw together all combinations of colors. It didn't matter. Scarlet red against dark purple against lizard green. Mom's conventional sewing background was not used to this mix.

"It looks like someone on a three-day drunk!" she would exclaim. "I'm not sure anyone could sleep under this quilt. It's too loud!" But we persisted. I had a secret fear that she might not even live to see the end result.

"Mama had a treadle machine when we kids were all still home, but she wouldn't let any of us touch it. She threatened to beat us if we did."

The pattern went together easily, and it was not long before we had produced several ten-inch wide by six-foot long strips of multi-colored chevrons. I clothes-pinned them to the top of the china closet. They hung down to the floor, psychedelic banners flying their freak flags in Mom's modest little house.

I found myself looking forward to pulling out the fabric and the old Singer every day. At first, I thought it was because I simply love sewing, and this was a great excuse to sew unencumbered, with no time limit. I didn't have a job to go to every day. I had very few obligations other than keeping an eye on Mom. We could sew in her dining room for hours, and who would care? But I know now it was because during our sewing times together, I gained back my mother. It provided blocks of time when we both relaxed. We were not battling her brain, its distortions, its deviousness. We weren't battling each other. It provided an opportunity for me to sit next to a person who was becoming more and more a stranger to me, but who, when we cut and sewed and ironed together, was about the closest thing I could get to my real mother.

The woman who had been absent for the last several years would return on those evenings, sitting contentedly at the table, chatting with me about colors, about sewing machines, reminding me of who she always would be in my heart. Here was the patient woman who taught a little girl to sew. With those lessons, she gave me a gift that lasted a lifetime, for sewing has given me great joy and satisfaction as I sewed for my own children, for friends, for my home.

Mornings, Mom would emerge from her bedroom and have no memory of our sewing project. As she rounded the corner into the dining room and the blazing strips came into view, she would ask, "Where did those come from?"

Then with a bit of clarity, "Did we make those? Are we making a quilt?" And finally, "It looks like someone's been on a three-day drunk!"

EIGHTEEN

SPRING PARK COFFEE shop has become a favorite for both local residents as well as people passing through town. The tables are usually full of small groups of people, the baristas busily concocting delicious beverages. The décor echoes the town's faded, Victorian feel. Heavy, dark, ornately carved settees with brown and burgundy velvets are positioned in conversation clusters. Chalkboards set in gold rococo frames hang on the walls, listing menu items, giving coffee trivia facts, and encouraging customers to "Like Us On Facebook." Windows are draped in floor-length burlap panels. The shop telephone is a reproduction from the early 1900s, a large wooden box with a black mouthpiece below the dial. Music is piped through a hidden speaker in an old phonograph. There's an odd smattering of magazines on a coffee table: *Handgunner, Gun World, American Iron* ("The #1 Motorcycle Magazine on the Newstand"), and *Elle Décor*. Something for everyone.

Several photographs taken in Green Cove Springs in the late 1800s hang on the walls. They have been enlarged and framed in old, whitewashed window frames, the perfect rustic yet chic touch. One print shows the stately Clarendon Hotel before it burned to the ground in 1900. It was a five-story beauty, with turrets, a dozen gables along the roofline, and gingerbread trim on the wrap-around porch. Dapper men pose in white waistcoats and straw hats, sporting handlebar mustaches; elegantly dressed women hold parasols and sip tea on the expansive front verandah. There's a photo taken around 1900 of the sulfur spring. Tourists stroll along a wooden boardwalk, framed by moss-draped trees and the river in the background. It's a sort of swampy, sepia version of Seurat's famous pointillist painting, *A Sunday Afternoon on the Island of La Grande Jatte.*

By far, my favorite photograph on the walls of the coffee shop is of three men, two dead alligators, and a dog. Two of the men stand holding rifles; the third grips a Bowie knife in his right hand, with the point casually planted on the tail of one of the alligators. Both gators are over ten feet long. The dog, a light-colored hound, is perched on the back of one of the dead alligators.

The men with the rifles seem dressed for a formal Sunday afternoon event: one is in a double-breasted jacket with brass buttons, and a boat-captain hat. The other man could have stepped out of a recent J. Crew photo shoot, wearing a turtleneck under a blazer, a small brimmed hat that would now be considered cool and retro, his hand resting on the shoulder of the dog. The third man with the knife seems to be the real outdoorsman: no jacket, his shirtsleeves rolled up to the elbow, his sweat-stained brimmed straw hat tilted back on his head. He has a bushy mustache and a quiet, stern look.

The alligators are laid out on makeshift tables – plywood boards balanced across wooden shipping crates. One gator's eye socket is obliterated by a dark bloody hole;

their mouths are clamped in deathly frozen smiles. With the exception of the alligators, the subjects in the photo look smug.

Alligator hunting was a profitable business in the late 1800s. Hunters poled their boats quietly along the banks of the river during the night, catching the reflections of red eyes in the dark. The spacing between the eyes indicated the size of the gator. The men would either stun the gators with a strong blow to the head, followed by a bullet to either the eye or ear, or simply take the shot right off with a .22 rifle. Good money was made from both the skins and the meat.

I imagine the rugged man with the knife guiding wealthy city slickers on nighttime gator hunts. He carefully maneuvered the boat among reeds under low-hanging branches, letting them pull the trigger after he spotted the monsters near the shore. Later they would haul their game back to shore and pose for a photograph to be sent to friends up north.

I love the juxtaposition of this gruesome scene against the elegant Victorian décor of the coffee shop. I think most people who stand in line to order a caramel macchiato or Peppermint Patty latte don't notice the photograph.

On one of my visits, I took a snapshot of it with my phone and posted it on my Facebook page. It was so iconic, perfectly capturing the Gothic and sometimes grotesque nature of things in this town. Almost immediately, my cousin Margaret commented on my posting: "Wanda! That is your great-great-grandfather in the white shirt!" The man

with the knife. His name was Alexander Bentley. I
remembered my mother talking about the Bentleys, but I
didn't know anything specific about that side of the family.
The Bentleys and Chessers intermarried after the Chessers
migrated from the Okefenokee Swamp into north Florida.

I returned to the coffee shop to ask where the
photograph came from.

"We got all of these images—the gator photo, the old
hotels—down at the county archives," Steve, the owner, tells
me. "They'll be happy to share any of their old photos with
you."

I drove back down to the archives at the old jail, and
Vishi very kindly searched through a number of files on her
computer, eventually pulling up the image. I copied it to a
thumb drive, thanking her for all her help. The papier-
mâché prisoner still hung quietly from the second-story
window over the parking lot as I drove away.

Later, I have a glossy black and white print made from
the image, put it in a frame, and place it on my desk. It
makes me proud. It's a daily reminder that I am descended
from a dragon-slayer.

NINETEEN

THE EASTERN STAR LAST RITES ceremony is full of symbolism and dignity. At the funeral of an Eastern Star member, a five-pointed star made of flowers, each point a different color, is placed near the casket. During the ceremony, Eastern Star members explain the symbolism of the five colors as a way to honor the deceased.

> *Blue is the color of friendship.*
> *It is a love expressed through faithfulness*
> *clear as a cloudless, cerulean sky.*

The Mount Pleasant Missionary Baptist Church is a beige painted cinderblock building on the corner of Martin Luther King Boulevard and West Street. The wake for Gregg's mother was on a Friday night. I parked in the sandy lot next to the church, under a large live oak tree. It was early November; the evening was pleasantly cool. Across the street from the church were houses and a playground, surrounded by a gray metal chain-link fence. Above the field, the sky was golden, filled with soft autumn evening light. The family assembled near the front steps of the church. People stood in clusters, talking quietly. Young parents reeled in restless children.

The funeral home hearse arrived. The casket was wheeled in, followed by Miss Helen's children, their spouses, grandchildren, nieces, nephews. The cool evening air drifted in through the open doors. The rest of us entered the church and found our seats.

The casket was at the front of the sanctuary, the large Eastern Star made of flowers was on a stand next to the casket. A man wearing a black suit and white gloves slowly lifted the heavy casket lid and pushed it open. The ivory-colored satin lining of the casket was gathered in tucks and pleats. It gleamed in the lights. The man gently, reverently reached in the casket and removed a small white lace handkerchief that was lying across Miss Helen's still face. He moved to the end of the casket and opened a tiny hidden door, pulled out a handle, and slowly turned it clockwise. Miss Helen, lying recumbent, was gradually raised up, a tiny dark wisp of a woman, her eyes closed, her lips closed. The man sat down and the service began.

The Grand Master took his place at the head of the casket and addressed the congregation. He spoke from memory, delivering an ancient-sounding and formal soliloquy.

"Brothers and sisters, we are now assembled around the final resting place of these mortal remains, to perform the final rites and solemn duties of respect that we owe to our departed friend and sister. A few reflections therefore are applicable to the solemnity of this occasion."

He continued. "This spot is hallowed with the memories of departed friendships, which linger around the heart, awakening a thousand melancholy and pleasing reflections. The lessons of her exemplary life linger in our remembrance and are reflected beyond the portals of the tomb. The floral emblem of the Eastern Star instructs us with an eloquence more powerful than words."

He motioned to a group of women who were sitting on the front pew.

"Sister Elector, Worthy Matrons, please come forward as representatives of the Five Heroines of the Eastern Star, and impart to us the significance of their beauty and remind us of the lessons they contain."

One by one, five women took their turns at the side podium, at the foot of the casket, and recited the lesson from each of the five colors in the star – red, yellow, blue, green, white.

Green is the color of immortality, of undeviating sincerity.

I've known Gregg since fourth grade. It was the first year of elementary school integration in our school system. Gregg, Beverly, and Melondia were the first African-American children I went to school with, my first black friends. Because our town was so small, all of us went to school together from elementary through high school. Friendships here run deep, long, and sometimes across multiple generations of families.

On the afternoon that my father passed away, Gregg was the first person to arrive at my mother's house. He found the closest restaurant open on a Sunday and brought fried chicken, potato salad and rolls. We ate together, and he sat with us in the living room for hours that day, while we waited for the Hospice nurse to drive down from Jacksonville, then Mr. Helm from the funeral home with a hearse and gurney, and finally the pastor from my mother's church.

Red is the color of fervency, unfading beauty.

Miss Helen's funeral service began at ten o'clock the next morning, the day after the wake. Gregg has fourteen siblings. They were raised by a single mother who instilled rock-solid values and a firm moral uprightness in her kids. Parents of just one child would be hard-pressed to duplicate what she accomplished with fifteen. But she did it, over and over. She was a tiny woman, strong-minded and strong-willed, a firecracker, a Legend.

The family, when seated, took up about half of the pews in the church. Ushers brought in folding chairs, setting them along the side aisles for the rest of us, but it wasn't enough. Dozens of people remained standing along the back wall of the sanctuary, in the foyer, outside on the sidewalk.

I saw many faces I recognized from my childhood. I saw Ruth, the woman who kept the nursery at the Methodist Church when I was an infant and toddler. Ruth would hold me in her lap and sing to me and tell me stories in the nursery's wooden rocking chair. She had large beautiful hands, and small black freckles across her brown face. She smelled clean and soothing, and spoke and laughed in a deep, rich voice. Ruth was the mother to a house full of children herself. The only children I remembered were the twin girls who were about five years older than me. Like their mother, they were tall, beautiful, with high cheekbones and broad, open smiles. At the funeral, the twins flanked Ruth, now slim and frail, holding and guiding her as she walked.

There were purple altar flowers, many women wore purple dresses, small purple ribbons were pinned to men's lapels. Three ministers presided over the service and each one gave a sermon. One of them was tall and slender as a rail, with a rumbling bass voice. His voice was powerful, compelling. "Do I hear the church say A-men? I say, do I *hear* the church say A-men?"

The choir sang several songs throughout the service. A woman from the choir stood and sang a solo. Her full alto voice filled the sanctuary, filled our souls. The organist not only accompanied the choir and the soloists, he provided melodic flourishes and embellishments throughout the sermons, emphasizing the preachers' words during brief pauses, with dramatic effect. An usher gathered the small cards from the many flower arrangements lining the front altar, and handed them to a woman as she walked up to the podium. The names and messages on every card were read out loud.

After the sermons and solos, we stood and waited as each pew was emptied into a line that moved to the front of the church, in order to view Miss Helen one final time. The line moved slowly. The family remained seated. Then we were all dismissed from the sanctuary, leaving the family and the ministers and Miss Helen.

It was almost two in the afternoon by now. The congregation waited patiently in the churchyard. There were people I knew in high school but had not seen at all in the years that had passed. We stood in clusters, catching up one another on our lives, telling shortened stories of jobs, siblings, children. The family emerged from the church about a half hour later. The casket was rolled out to the waiting hearse. The cemetery was just up the street, so most of us walked along the sidewalk in a quiet procession to the gravesite, where we said our final goodbyes to Miss Helen.

White is the color of truth and innocence, purity and joy. A pure life lived brings happiness now and in the life beyond.

When Gregg's mother's health started declining, he moved back to her house to care for her. We often compared notes about caring for our mothers. His mother would not feel well enough to eat, so he cajoled and pleaded and reasoned with her with endless patience, until he could get her to try a few bites of food. When I complained to him about the latest frustrating thing with mom, he would always encourage me. "Wanda, you just gotta take it easy with her. I do it that way with my mom. I try a little bit at a time. It's hard, but try to be patient." I would never have the patience that he had.

One of the battles that Mom's caregivers and I fought practically every week was over her bathing. She consistently refused to bathe. As was true in a lot of situations with Mom, no amount of calm reasoning or polite requests were effective.

I would usually start with, "Mom, it has been a week since you showered," or "Mom, you need to bathe because you have a doctor's appointment this afternoon," or sometimes the harshest indictment of all, "Mom, you smell like urine."

"My grandmother almost never took baths, and she was one of the cleanest women I knew," would be her comeback, every time.

Even though I knew it was pointless, it was hard for me not to be pulled into the argument. "Mom, the reason she didn't bathe was that she didn't have access to indoor plumbing. If she had endless hot water like you do, I bet she would have bathed three times a day."

She couldn't argue with that, but at the same time, my logic never once got her to go into the bathroom and shower. She would dismiss me with a wave of her hand and walk out of the room.

Over time, I noticed something about my mother's behavior, and eventually, at least a few times, I was able to leverage it. She would not bathe for me nor for her caregivers. But when I made plans to take her out of the house for an appointment or to a restaurant for a meal, she would always ask, "Will there be men there?" Followed by,

"Maybe I'll meet a man while we're out! I would love to have someone to go out with."

And so I learned to reply, "Well, in case we run into any men, you probably should shower and be fresh and clean." It worked, at least on and off for a couple of years. She would throw down the bath-time gauntlet, always forgetting that I had the man-card in my back pocket.

Then one day a new tactic emerged. Gregg stopped by for a visit. He loved my Mom, called her his "second mom." And she loved him. They were sitting together on her sofa, chatting, repeating the same conversational topics over and over. I brought Gregg a glass of tea and sat in the chair opposite them.

"I've been trying all morning to get her to go shower, but she's refusing," I confessed in a quiet voice to Gregg, knowing that she could not hear our sideline conversation. "It's been four days," I whispered.

Without any hesitation, Gregg turned to her with a surprised look on his face. "Miss Juanita! When is the last time you showered?" he asked pointedly.

Mom looked a little surprised. "Oh, well, I showered this morning. Or...I might have showered last night." She looked over at me for some kind of confirmation. I sat mute and stone-faced. "I shower every day, of course!" she laughed, incredulous at the implication.

"OK, then," Gregg responded. "I think you told me that you were waiting until two o'clock today to get your shower, and look at this!" He pointed to his wristwatch. "It's two o'clock on the dot! You be a good girl and go shower, and I'll wait here on the couch until you are out."

And she did. She got up off the couch, excused herself, and a few minutes later we could hear the shower running. After that, I tried to catch Gregg when he wasn't busy, to stop by the house and exclaim to Mom that it was two o'clock on the dot, and time for that shower!

Yellow is the color of kindness.
Kindness is love that shines like the yellow rays of the sun.

It is a Saturday night in June, Mom and I have finished supper, it's getting dark outside. Gregg calls me.

"Hey. What're you doing?" Gregg has a deep voice, almost a growl. "Come over to the house. Ivan's having a party, mostly family. C'mon over."

Gregg lives in his mother's house now that she has passed. It's a few blocks from my mother's house. I drive up into the front yard, past the birdbath and white angel statue that were his mother's. A circle of rocks surround the birdbath, all painted white. I park my car in the yard. There are probably a dozen other cars pulled up in rows between the house and the street.

A floodlight shines down in front of a metal-roofed structure. Fabric mosquito netting hangs on all four sides. There are a couple of tables and a recliner inside, coolers sitting on the concrete slab, a table with food set up in the middle. Men and women are mingling around, drinking, eating from Styrofoam plates. "Harpo's Place" is hand lettered on a large sign, hanging from a metal pole. There are three wooden picnic tables outside, two of them covered in large picnic-sized foil pans filled with fried fish, pulled pork barbecue, grilled chicken, slaw, potato salad, corn on the cob, macaroni salad. Tortilla chips spill from bags, a row of empty beer bottles stands on the edge of one table. Two grills are set up to the side. Dennis, one of Gregg's brothers, and a friend are sitting together at one of the picnic tables, drinking beer and peeling shrimp.

I walk over and see another brother, Ivan. He's holding a large Styrofoam Sonic cup.

"I'm surprised you're drinking a Sonic drink at your own party!"

"I got stuff in here that I didn't get from Sonic," he grins. "So how do you like Harpo's Place?"

"This is great, Ivan. Where did the name come from?"

"There was a joint in the movie *The Color Purple* called Harpo's Place. I named it after that."

"Gregg called me and invited me over. Where is he?" I asked.

"He's at the house, cooking." Ivan offers me a beer from an ice chest. I pull out a bottle and walk back across the yard. I step up onto the screened front porch of the old frame house.

"Hey, you!" I holler into the living room. The house looks like Miss Helen is still there. Everything is so tidy. Framed photographs of family members hang on the walls and line the tops of chests and bookshelves.

Gregg hollers back, "Now, I wonder who could that be? Who's come poking around here?" He emerges from the kitchen laughing, his tall frame filling the doorway. "I'm cooking my rice and I can't let it burn. Nobody cooked no rice for this thing, so I told Ivan I would just fix my own and bring it." Still grinning, he walks across the living room to give me a hug.

I follow him back into the kitchen. Once the rice is finished, Gregg secures a lid on it and carries it out of the house using two dishtowels as hot mitts. We walk toward the party in the dark, across the grass, Gregg holding the steaming pot high as he sidles between parked cars. We pass a car tag nailed diagonally to a shed wall: "Jesus is so precious to me."

An old white Chevy Caprice is pulled up next to Harpo's on the grass. Its doors are wide open, music blaring from the car speakers. Gregg sets down his pot, and we walk around the table to get our plates and load up on food. He pointed over to the area next to the picnic tables. There was a small brick patio. "That's the dance floor. Ivan is still working on it, and he wants to put in a fountain, too."

The night deepens, the party gets louder. Everyone mingles, some of us try a few rounds of the Electric Slide on the brick dance floor. About every third word uttered by a lot of the men seems to be "mother-fuckin'," even the polite ones who are in the church choir every Sunday morning and were raised by Helen Williams. There is lots of laughter, lots of good-natured kidding.

At some point I move to the edge of the party, and I think I hear the hooting of an owl. I follow the sound back to where the cars are parked in front of Gregg's house. I see a faint light in a tree. As I move closer, I see that it's a solar-powered landscaping light, the kind that normally lines sidewalks and driveways, stuck out at an angle about eight feet off the ground in the branches of a crepe myrtle. I hear the hooting again. Nearby, perched on a utility line that spans the yard, two juvenile owls, fluffy and brown, and an adult owl are all backlit by a street lamp.

Train tracks run along the back line of Gregg's property, just yards from the rear of the house. Several times during the party, trains pass by. The distant warning horn blows as the trains approach town. It's a sound so common here that most people don't notice it. The rumbling gets closer. I feel it in my feet. Being outside in the dark, so close to the tracks, the coming trains sound menacing, growing louder and closer. As we stand in the yard, talking, eating, drinking, the trains blast past like enormous storms barreling through the dark trees behind the house. Everyone pauses in their conversations for a few seconds. A black blur of motion and noise, small yellow squares flying by in the trees for just a few moments, then it's gone. People resume their conversations. The ground under my feet vibrates well after the final red light on the last car fades down the track. There are faces behind those yellow squares, people speeding through the dark. No one on the trains aware of the backyards they slice through, the lives that they pass by so closely in the Florida night.

CHILDREN'S DAY AT CASINO, GREEN COVE SPRINGS, FLA   *a : K . B*   E. C. KROPP CO., MILWAUKEE

TWENTY

The water boils up from a large fissure at the rate of three thousand gallons per minute. It is as clear as a diamond, and the effect is most beautiful at noonday, when the sun shines directly into the spring, and objects can be seen at the bottom tinted with the prismatic hues.

THE POCKET DIRECTORY OF GREEN COVE SPRINGS, 1889

I HAD MY PALM read once in college. It was the May Day festival on campus. Food vendors and activities were set up on the plaza outside the Student Union building. My friend Julia and I had our caricatures drawn by one of those on-the-fly artists. The sketch of Julia perfectly captured her personality: an open, laughing face, big smile, a sparkle in her eyes. Mine? I couldn't see any resemblance. I wasn't sure if the artist had even looked at me while drawing, or if he just absent-mindedly put together some generic female features on the sheet of paper while he flirted with Julia.

We moved on to the palm reader. Julia's reading was as I expected. Her life would be full of adventure and excitement. She and the reader gazed at the miracle unfolding in the lines of Julia's left palm. Romance, intrigue, international travel. Then the reader took my hand, turning it this way and that in the afternoon sunshine. Finally, sounding a little relieved that there was something to say, she pointed out that the star-shaped lines under my ring finger indicated a significant life event, and that my lifeline was long. So far, so good.

Then she stated confidently, "You are a swimmer."

"No," I replied, always embarrassed when this topic comes up. "I never learned to swim, even though I grew up in Florida."

She seemed undaunted. "Well, I see a strong connection to water. Your life is closely tied to water in some way." She was unwavering, insistent.

This woman was clearly a fake, and the whole experience confirmed the silliness of palm reading. If I had not learned to swim by this point, there was no hope I would ever become a "water person." Julia and I walked back to our dorm, the palm reading gone from my mind about as quickly as my caricature was tossed into the trashcan.

I always regretted that I never learned to swim. It surprises people who meet me and find out that I am from Florida, and that I did not naturally become a swimmer straight out of the womb. Everyone who lives in Florida is a swimmer, right? It's a stereotype I've heard all of my life.

My parents did their part. They dutifully sent me to swim lessons at the city pool when I was four or five. I was just tall enough to stand in the shallow end, the cold water in the early summer morning air all the way up to my chin. I didn't get it. Letting go of terra firma, being surrounded by something that didn't allow me to breathe did not seem like a good idea. I didn't like getting water up my nose and burning my throat. I didn't like the idea of drowning right here in the shallow end of my hometown pool and making a spectacle of myself. I was terrified and I must have created quite a fuss, because I didn't go back after the first lesson.

I spent my childhood mostly on dry land, while other kids, normal kids born in Florida who began swimming right out of the womb, swam at pool parties, the beach, the lake. I knew I was missing out on something special. I didn't know how I would ever be able to get past my fear of deep water, and be like all those other kids.

When I was twelve, I saw a TV interview with some of the Weeki Wachee mermaids. They were so beautiful, so elegant, so magical. Gliding effortlessly underwater, they performed graceful acrobatics, enchanting audiences in shimmering swirls of glitter and fins and hair and bubbles. They discreetly sipped air from little tubes, smiling all the while. Of course I wanted to be like them.

The reporter posed the question, "How old were you when you started swimming with the mermaids?"

"I was twelve," replied one of the gorgeous creatures.

Twelve! Just my age! There might yet be hope for me to learn to swim, if mermaids didn't learn until they were my age!

"Mom, did you hear that? She didn't learn to swim until she was twelve!"

"Sweetie, I think she means that she already knew how to swim, and she learned the diving part at twelve."

That sealed the deal. I had missed my chance to be a swimmer. And I would certainly never be able to swim like the mermaids.

I took swim lessons as an adult once. I was able to float curled up in a ball for a few seconds, which seemed like an eternity, leaving me panicked and gasping. So I spent my adulthood on dry land as well, declining invitations to pool parties, never venturing beyond the shallow end in any pool. *Learn to swim!* has been on many of my New Year's resolution lists, year after year, never crossed off.

Being back in Green Cove, I eye the city pool with a wish that turned into resolve. I look at that wall along the shallow end and remember my four-year-old self, the feeling of fear and hesitation. I watch a few YouTube videos on adult beginning swim lessons and return to the pool of my childhood, determined to become comfortable in the water. The first day I go, it is a hot July afternoon and thankfully the pool is almost empty. I ease into the water and it takes my breath away. Seventy-eight degree water feeding from the natural spring sounds balmy, but it's actually about ten degrees colder than a typical swimming pool. I keep moving, determined not to make a fool of myself. The water is crystal clear and oh-so-cold. But I'm adjusting as I walk, water up to my waist, then slowly to my shoulders. I dip to my chin and it's okay. It feels good. I can do this.

I start by simply walking laps in the shallow end, back and forth, back and forth. Becoming friends with the water. Next, I hold on to a blue pool noodle, trying out the sensation of floating and kicking. Eventually I abandon the noodle and push off, flutter kick for a few seconds, my face above the water. Over and over I do this simple move, hands forward, flutter kick, breaststroke, head above the water.

After a while it's not too difficult, not scary. Of course, I'm still in the shallow end. I recall that I did float on my back in adult swim class decades ago, so I try that. It's a miracle. I lie back and gaze at the sky, my back arched, the water supporting me, and I can breathe. I am floating in the same place where the tourists came to "take to the water" in an elegant glass-covered pool over a hundred years ago. I'm a kid again in this pool, making up for all those years of not swimming.

The water is so fresh, no chemicals. Beautiful, clear, delicious sulfur water, straight up from the earth. I want to open my mouth and gulp the water while I paddle around. I am surrounded by water that tastes and smells like home, water that comes from the Fountain of Youth. And what a setting. Looking past the deep end of the pool, I see the blue St. Johns River and beyond, all the way to the shoreline of the opposite bank.

I'm beginning to understand something about being in the water. I float better when I am not thrashing, when I am not struggling to gasp for breath, hurrying to get to the edge. I relax, pulling through the water slowly, slowly. My body cooperates and bobs to the surface. My arms gracefully push through the water, silvery bubbles flying off my fingertips. I am not a true swimmer yet. Far from it. But just for a minute there, I think I caught a glimpse of my inner mermaid.

TWENTY-ONE

JUST PAST HILLTOP, as you drive west on Highway 16 out of town, is Hickory Grove Cemetery. The cemetery is on both sides of the highway. Graves in the old section, on the right side of the road, date to the early 1800s. Narrow mossy headstones lean in the shade; the grass is tall, some headstones are toppled, lying flat and forgotten. First names inscribed on the stones—Ozias and Marmaduke and Caleb—are like a whisper from a forgotten time. Across the road, more giant, gnarled live oaks line the drive into the newer section of the cemetery, the trees draped with grey Spanish moss as if placed there by mourning angels. The dirt drive is sandy and littered with pine needles and scraps of flattened moss. The oldest graves are the first ones along the drive, many are in aboveground crypts, gray boxes huddled together in the shade of old trees. The drive curves, the graveyard becomes open and flat, tall pines along the far perimeter. Gray granite memorials stand as sentinels in family plots, family names in large black letters visible from a distance. The cemetery seems to be its own little town, with neighborhoods of familiar names.

Visits from the living become evident as you drive further in. Silk poinsettias, once red and cheery from some far-removed Christmas, are now faded to splotches of white and pink. They lean wearily against headstones or lie in the grass, forgotten. There are wind chimes, bejeweled dragonflies, plastic iridescent butterflies, ladybugs. Strands of plastic Mardi Gras beads and garlands of seashells drape headstones. Solar-powered landscape lights sprout from the ground like dandelions. A menagerie of concrete yard art—deer, alligators, dogs—pose next to and on graves. There are as many types of modern-day physical mementos here as there are families in this county. Praying hands. NASCAR hotrods. A plastic pig with wings. A brass trumpet. And of course, all manner of angels. Praying angels, angels holding Bibles, bouquets of flowers, candles. It's a kind of outdoor museum for sacred yard art.

On the back drive is Babyland, marked by a small lettered sign hammered into the grass. A toddler's grave from decades ago is strewn with dozens of small faded plastic cars. Alongside the cars are other random toys and figurines: two angels kissing, a rotting green foam soccer ball, a baby rattle in the shape of a rabbit, a rubber millipede. All are covered with a light sprinkling of brown pine needles and sit among white gravel on the tiny grave. At another grave, a hollow ceramic cherub dozes, its legs cracked open, full of soil. There are clowns and angels, and ghosts of grayed-out stuffed animals left to rot in the weather.

Years passed after my father's death and I never bothered to go to the cemetery at all. Now I usually go when I'm in town. Late-life penance, I suppose. I drive past the white cement columns, taking the slow route around the winding sandy drive. I pass Chessers, Owens, Bentleys, Knowles, Lees. I deliberately go the long way. My father's grave is in the far back section, only a few rows from the rear border of tall pines.

The headstone that my mother picked out for Dad's grave has dogwood blossoms engraved on it. She selected it to honor his birth state, since the dogwood is North Carolina's state flower. When I finally returned to the cemetery, brown mold had grown deep in the crevices of the dogwood blossoms. I went back with a bucket and scrub brush, trying to amend the years of neglect. I never asked Mom about it, but I'm sure it had been years since she visited as well.

Now when I'm at his grave, I usually have something on my mind that I want to say to Dad.

Dad, Mom is really not well, and she's struggling, and I miss you so much. And she misses you, too.

Dad, Bill is gone. I guess you know. I don't even know where to start. I don't know what to do. I wish you were here to talk to. I miss you so much.

After five years of caregivers, trips back and forth between North Carolina and Florida, and increasing concern about Mom's ability to stay in her home, my brother and I made the decision to move her back to North Carolina, into a nursing home. I drove out to the cemetery. I stood at the foot of the Dad's gravesite, avoiding the gray sand mounds of anthills, watching to make sure the stinging red ants didn't find my feet and start up my ankles.

Dad, I'm moving Mom to North Carolina. I need to have her close to me. She still loves you so much, and I do, too.

How ironic that my father was born in North Carolina, that most of his family stayed there, lived and died there, and here he lies in a grave five hundred miles away. And now I am moving my mother away from her home, five hundred miles north, likely never to see Florida again.

In the distance, on the western boundary of the cemetery, a hawk circled high, dropping quickly, swooping, its gray silhouette against the dark pines. It was chasing a dove, the two of them careening and dancing, around and around. The dove kept ahead; they darted out of sight over the trees, then back out again, the dove's wingbeats quick and sure, clipping furiously in the afternoon sunshine. It was life or death. Nothing else. There was, for that dove, no future and no past. Just now, just this. The present. Life. Death. Against a bright afternoon sky.

TWENTY-TWO

To all we would say, come and see for yourself, and you will be fully convinced that there is but one Green Cove Springs, and that it is the most beautiful and delightful retreat for the invalid or the tired traveler who may seek rest or a home.

THE POCKET DIRECTORY OF GREEN COVE SPRINGS, 1889

I OFTEN THINK OF how my mother, the mother I had known all of my life, ceased to exist in her last eight years. Walking through life with a dementia patient is like going through two deaths. The confusion, the lack of functioning, day after day, month after month, erased my real mother before she was physically gone. Sometimes it was hard to remember the woman she had been for the majority of my life.

The nursing home seemed to be good for her. She enjoyed having more social contact, she ate better, and even had a boyfriend. She and Norm would sit together in the common living room on Sunday afternoons, watching NFL football, holding hands. When I learned that Norm had died, the sting of my own grief surprised me. I didn't even know his last name. Mom didn't remember his existence at all. I suppose I grieved for her, because she couldn't. Mom lived for three more years after the move, and died from heart failure at age eighty-six.

After her death, I took stock of where I was, made some changes, and decided to live part time in her little house in Green Cove Springs, at least for a while.

I miss my mother every day, and especially because I live in her home and she is not here. I bought curtains for the living room window, and after they were hung I realized I'd bought the same style and color that she chose for that window. The bedroom closet was dark, so I rigged up a florescent light with an extension cord into the closet, then remembered that she had the same type of contraption set up, in the same closet. I think about her when I pass by the old theatre, when I sew, when I see that gator photo on the wall of the coffee shop.

On a late summer evening I walk to the park. A thunderstorm skirts west of town, the sky in that direction a beautifully textured canvas, filled with purples, oranges, pinks and grays. An occasional thread of lightning jumps among the clouds in the far distance. Following the meandering sidewalk through the park, I make my way to the pier. Despite the storm in the west, the sky directly overhead remains blue, filled with long straight streaks of white-gray clouds, extending to the eastern horizon across the river.

It's shrimping season, late July. Both sides of the pier are lined with clusters of people, some casting large circular nets into the river, some smoking, a few sitting in folding lawn chairs. As the sky darkens, streetlights flicker on, casting an artificial blue tint on the concrete pier. Children scamper about, squealing, picking up dead and dying minnows next to the tangled wet slumps of empty nets. Several groups of families are staked along the railing together. There's raucous laughter and the crisp sweet smell of cigarette smoke on the breeze. An old battery-operated radio plays country music.

I walk along slowly, sidestepping blue plastic coolers and bait buckets, puddles with tangled lines and silvery fish heads. Near the end of the pier, I find an empty spot where I lean on the railing and watch the glistening water.

An old woman sits alone on an upturned plastic milk crate, watching the bobber of her fishing pole dance on the water's surface. Her fuzzy gray hair puffs out from under a faded baseball cap. She's short, heavy-set, wearing a black tank top and cut-off jeans. On one wrist is a black leather bracelet with metal studs, her other arm is wrapped with a soiled fabric brace. She stands up and gathers her things to move to another spot on the pier.

As she passes me, she smiles with a snaggle-toothed grin and says, "It's the best place for good thinking." I smile in return. She shuffles away, dragging her pole and milk crate, leaving me with my thoughts, watching the black water rippling below.

Later that night, I push open the window at the head of my bed, just an inch or two. Outside, the fronds in the palmetto tree clatter in the warm breeze. I turn out the light and place my pillow close to the windowsill. The familiar damp, earthy smell floats in the window, lingering with the metallic odor from the old screen that keeps out the mosquitoes.

Lying in bed, I listen to the trains rumble through town, their whistles blowing forlornly. The first blast, a major triad, is easy and gentle. I wonder about the person pulling the lever that sounds the horn. What do they see as they pass through this quiet town? The groans of the horns are strung together like dark pearls on a long string. I count the blasts: the whistle blows twenty-four, twenty-five, twenty-six times.

After the sounds fade, I feel the deep thrum of the train engines in my chest, a heavy purring rhythm. Some nights, depending on the direction of the wind, it's as if the train passes only yards from my window. One train dissolves away, I begin to drift into sleep, and another train cries out on its approach. It is hard for me to believe I have spent my entire adult life without hearing these train symphonies every night, the blending of the horn tones, spilling out across the sleeping town, seeping into the ground.

Caring for my mother at the end of her life was exhausting, frustrating, sad. But the town, the trains, the brick streets, the river, the spring, the presence of old friends—they provided solace. A balance to the dismay of watching my mother decline. A century and a half ago, the town held a promise of restorative, healing powers for the weary and the sick. When I returned to Green Cove Springs, it kept its promise.

My mind wanders back to the river. It's very late now. No shrimpers on the dock, no fishermen on the river in metal johnboats. I imagine the tide lapping against the low concrete sea walls in the dark, the shift and tug on the tall grasses and cattails at the river's edge. Empty Styrofoam cups and beer cans tangled in the grasses, swaying with the tide, gleaming in the moonlight. Maybe a bullfrog's rasping grunts call out from the reeds. Maybe an alligator's bellow echoes from the shallows. The Great Blue Heron sleeps, leggy and folded like an antique umbrella, hidden among the branches of a cedar tree in the park.

The sounds of the trains fade as they make the final sweeping curve south of town, where the old depot once stood, the last clearing before the tracks disappear into the black piney-wood night.

ABOUT THE AUTHOR

WANDA SUTTLE DUNCAN earned her Bachelor's degree at Catawba College in Salisbury, North Carolina, and her Master of Arts in Liberal Studies degree at Wake Forest University, where her academic focus was on Southern literature and creative non-fiction. She has been a contributing writer to *The Digital Forsyth Project*, *Early American Music Magazine*, and *Our State Magazine*, the state magazine for North Carolina. She was the recipient of the 2018 Library Partners Press David Coates Non-Fiction Award.

Cracker Gothic: A Florida Woman's Memoir is her first book.

Made in the USA
Columbia, SC
23 April 2019